Keep the Buttered Side Up

FOOD SUPERSTITIONS FROM AROUND THE WORLD

WHOOPS!

KATHLYN GAY

ILLUSTRATIONS BY
DEBBIE PALEN

WALKER AND COMPANY
NEW YORK

First published in the United States of America
in 1995 by Walker Publishing Company, Inc.

Published simultaneously in Canada by
Thomas Allen & Son Canada, Limited, Markham, Ontario

Library of Congress Cataloging-in-Publication Data
Gay, Kathlyn.
Keep the buttered side up : food superstitions from around the
world / Kathlyn Gay : illustrations by Debbie Palen.
    p. cm.
ISBN 0-8027-8228-0 (hardcover). — ISBN 0-8027-7469-5
(paperback)
1. Food—Folklore. 2. Food habits—Folklore. 3. Food—
Symbolic aspects—Juvenile literature. [1. Food—Folklore. 2.
Food habits—Folklore.] I. Palen, Debbie, ill. II. Title.
          GR498.G39   1995
          398'.355—dc20
          95-13012
          CIP
          AC

Book design by Eddy Herch

Printed in the United States of America
2 4 6 8 10 9 7 5 3 1

TABLE OF CONTENTS

Keep the Buttered Side Up

Keep the Buttered Side Up

"ONE FOR THE BLACKBIRD..."

One for the blackbird,
One for the crow,

One for the cutworm,
And two to let it grow.

MANY A FARMER OR HOME GARDENER is familiar with the above chant, used when planting seeds of corn. Early colonizers in the Americas repeated the incantation, which they had adapted from a superstitious custom of people native to the land. Whereas Native Americans had always planted four kernels of corn in each hill, North American colonists planted five kernels, in the belief that by providing for the blackbird, crow, and cutworm, and by adding another seed for luck, they could ensure that the fifth would grow. A similar superstitious chant has accompanied the planting of beans: "One for the rook, one for the crow; one to die, and one to grow."

Although today's farmers and gardeners in industrialized nations use a great number of modern agricultural methods to ensure a good crop, planting, growing, and harvesting are affected by the many whims of nature. So some growers still follow superstitious practices—just in case technology needs a little help.

Descriptions of planting and harvesting superstitions fill pages of books, but some of the most basic have to do with favorable times for sowing or gathering crops. Those who heed the lunar cycle say that a full moon is a lucky time for planting corn. Crops that grow above-ground should be planted when the moon is waning, or getting smaller. When the moon is waxing—becoming larger—this signals the time for planting root crops, such as potatoes, carrots, and onions.

Certain days are auspicious also, such as Valentine's Day for planting peas and St. Patrick's Day for planting potatoes. Planting parsley on Good Friday guarantees a good crop until September, say some gardeners, who may also insist that "pole beans" be planted on that day, too.

The first day of May is the time many farmers and gardeners plant cucumbers, but the cucumbers are said to grow best if planted by a virile young man, preferably naked. According to garden lore, a redhead is the best person to plant carrots

and hot red peppers. Just about anyone can plant potatoes, but how you put them in the ground determines their fate: Potatoes should be planted with their eyes facing toward the surface, or how will they see to grow? And one ought to tie straw around the trunks of fruit trees on Christmas Eve in order to have a good crop the next year, says an old superstition.

A centuries-old practice in England is *wassailing*—offering toasts and drinking to a fruitful year. Farmers and townspeople toasted trees with cups of cider or glasses of wine, throwing the beverage at a particular tree or pouring it on the tree's roots while singing or chanting for "hatfuls, capfuls, three bushel bagsful" of fruit. Another form of the ritual was to soak toast in cider and place it in the fork of a tree branch for luck. After the toasting, townspeople fired shotguns into the tree branches to scare off any evil spirits that might be lurking around waiting to do damage to the crop.

Some say crops predict the weather. Gardeners in the southern part of the United States warn: Don't burn okra pods after they shed their seeds, because that could cause a drought. Onion skins may also be weather forecasters:

Onion's skin very thin,
Mild winter coming in.
Onion's skin thick and tough
Coming winter cold and rough.

Other harvesting superstitions stem from practices that have taken place since before recorded history. All around the world, ancient tribal groups held celebrations to present part of a harvest as a sacrifice or token of thanksgiving to the gods or goddesses who were thought to control the life cycles of plants and animals.

Today's harvest festivals carry on that custom. In the United States, for example, the Thanksgiving celebration usually includes a traditional meal of roasted turkey and pumpkin pie. The turkey, folklorists tell us, was the main dish for the harvest festival held by Mayans four thousand years ago. The Mayans also watched a ball game similar to American football in an enclosed courtyard somewhat like a football field. So if you're a football fan attending a game or watching games on TV, your Thanksgiving day is even more traditional!

As for the pumpkin pie, it could have ties to long-ago thanksgiving celebrations in Rome where the pumpkin was thought to represent the sun and its life-giving force. Thus it was an important symbol for harvest feasts. Before the Romans, however, Native Americans may have cultivated a squash that today we call the pumpkin, and celebrated it in harvest festivals.

Because food and water are basic to human survival, it is not surprising that people have developed superstitious beliefs and magical practices in this regard. Some are associated with crop and animal production; others are linked to preparation and use of specific foods and beverages. Many food and drink superstitions came about because of life ceremonies connected with such events as births and weddings, or because people established social customs and status symbols around eating or abstaining from certain foods. White bread, for example, was once a symbol of prosperity because it was expensive to process and bleach flour to make it lighter than the natural color of the wheat; dark bread made from unprocessed wheat was considered only suitable for the poor.

The use of bread for symbolic and magical purposes began with rituals that focused on the harvesting of corn and wheat, which provided the ground meal or flour for making bread. Bread has been called the "staff of life," and many people worldwide depend on some form of bread to fulfill their basic food needs. That may be one reason why bread, perhaps more than any other food, is surrounded by superstition, myth, and symbolism.

KEEP THE BUTTERED SIDE UP

"A loaf of bread," the Walrus said,
"Is what we chiefly need:
Pepper and vinegar besides
Are very good indeed —

Now if you're ready, Oysters dear,
We can begin to feed."
— Lewis Carroll,
Through the Looking-Glass

Day-old Bread

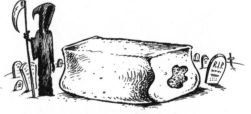

Dead Bread

FIRST, BE FOREWARNED: BAD LUCK is frequently associated with bread. Some people believe, for example, that if a baker sings before making bread, she or he will cry before the bread is eaten. If a huge hole appears in the middle of a baked loaf of bread, take care. It might portend a grave for someone.

Have you ever broken a sandwich in half to share with a friend or someone in your family? Well, watch where you break it. Breaking bread in someone's hand supposedly brings

bad luck. But be sure you do break—but never *cut*— the first loaf of bread that comes out of the oven; it's unlucky to cut it.

Still one more superstition cautions not to eat freshly baked bread— just out of the oven— because immediate misfortune will befall you. If true, there must be a lot of bad luck floating around: Thousands of loaves of freshly baked bread are now commonly served with restau-rant meals. And what about the countless pizza breads, hot and piled with toppings, that are sold and eaten daily? The purveyors are probably thanking their lucky stars. The only bad luck consumers may experience is indigestion from overeating.

If you buy a loaf of unsliced bread, be sure to store it rounded side up. Turning it upside down could signal the death of someone close to you, trouble for

How much pizza bread do Americans consume every day? Enough to fill ninety acres, or sixty-eight football fields.

a ship at sea, or an invitation for the devil to visit you. Such superstitions came about long ago when England and Scotland were at war. Apparently an English officer used an upside-down loaf of bread as a signal for a sneak attack on the Scots. So who can blame Scottish citizens for believing that upside-down bread brings harm?

Perhaps the British attack signal led to another sign of bad luck—dropping a piece of buttered bread on the floor. If it falls buttered side up, you and the bread are in good shape (not to mention your floor!). But a slice of bread smacking buttered side down is no joke. Not only do you have to clean up the mess, you also have to worry—if you're superstitious and the fretful type—about some adversity in the future.

Burned bread, it is said, will bring calamity upon your head. But you don't have to worry about this if your automatic toaster works well. The crumbs at the bottom of the toaster, which sometimes burn, don't

TIDBIT

What are the top three sandwich favorites among American schoolkids? Turkey heads the list, then comes ham, while peanut butter and jelly is a third-place choice, according to a survey of four thousand elementary school children conducted by a sandwich bag company.

count—unless someone throws them out and brings on an ancient curse of famine. Now, that's a good excuse for not cleaning out the toaster frequently.

And don't, for fortune's sake, leave a knife in an unsliced loaf of bread. You could be stabbing the source of your blessings! By the same reasoning, a woman should not stab a slice of bread on a fork or knife and pass it to someone else. An old British ditty warns: "She that pricks bread with a fork or knife/Will never be a happy maid or wife."

(There is no warning for men.)

Another superstition cautions that people who cut bread in unequal slices are announcing that they are habitual liars (although some of these individuals could just have poor eyesight). If you customarily slice off both ends of a whole loaf of bread, you might want to reconsider the practice. Cajuns in Louisiana say that cutting off both ends of a loaf before eating the middle means you may not be able to make ends meet; in other words, you could have problems paying your bills. So to play it safe, keep one crusty heel intact until you finish the loaf.

If you believe in the sorcery of the Middle Ages, you won't give that crust of bread to a stranger (bad luck, of course). Instead, to ensure good fortune, save the heel for a family member. It's an added plus if that family member yearns for curly hair—eating bread crusts supposedly curls the hair.

For another lucky attribute, consider keeping that crust. A crust of bread in your pocket or under your pillow at night could bring you prosperity or act as a charm to ward off danger and death, or so Europeans believed during the 1500s and 1600s. With a bread crust under your pillow, you are likely to dream of bread,

in which case you will experience happiness.

Bread also may increase your chances for a long life if you follow the age-old practice of passing bread around your table at mealtime. When you "break bread," or share bread, with strangers, you can expect, according to superstition, to establish friendships. This timeworn practice has gone beyond superstition, however, because people in many nations and cultures socialize by breaking bread, or eating together, and are likely to make friends or enhance friendships in this manner.

Breaking bread has been a lucky practice in other ways. During the 1700s in Scotland, for example, the eldest villager was always selected to carry a plate of small shortbread pieces into the home of a new bride. There, as a good luck gesture, the village elder dumped the pieces of bread over the bride's head as she came through the doorway. If any bridesmaid waiting outside could capture one of the scattered pieces of shortbread, she would be lucky in love and would quickly find a husband. In some parts of Europe years ago, it was a custom to put a piece of bread in a bride's shoe. This ensured that the marriage would produce many children, since bread was a symbol of fertility.

BREAD CUSTOMS AND RITUALS

• Unleavened bread is a traditional part of the Jewish seder, or Passover feast, celebrating the Israelites' flight from Egyptian bondage thousands of years ago. While the seder consists of a variety of foods that symbolize the Exodus, unleavened bread is a significant part of the entire eight-day Passover observance. As the term indicates, unleavened bread is made without a leaven, a substance that causes fermentation and makes dough rise. During Passover, many Jews refrain from eating any leaven as a reminder that the Israelites fled Egypt in great haste—with no time to wait for their bread dough to rise: "And the people took their dough before it was leavened, their kneading troughs being bound up in their clothes upon their shoulders . . . and they journeyed . . . and they baked unleavened cakes of the dough which they brought forth out of Egypt."[1]

• Italians have a near-sacred bond with bread—nearly every city and village in Italy boasts a bread or pastry made to its own specifications! Bread has been significant in Italian life ever since the days of ancient Rome, when it was believed that a special goddess, named Fornax, stood watch over the ovens. Each year, Romans honored Fornax by placing flowers above or on top of the ovens. Today, Italians make breads for every occasion, whether a holiday, wedding, or funeral, and consume 4.5 billion pounds of bread annually.[2]

• Historians and folklorists have tried to establish the origin of hot cross buns and trace their historical path. Some say the cross on the bun originated with ancient Greeks, who marked breadlike

cakes with a horned symbol and offered the baked goods to a goddess of love and fertility. Others claim the practice of marking bread with a cross stemmed from early Christian culture and the commemoration of Christ's death on a cross. Since that time, many European bread bakers have marked a cross in bread dough before baking, believing the symbol would protect both the bread and the household from evil. Thus, many historians conclude, hot cross buns stem from Christian tradition and today are part of meals served from Good Friday through Easter. In Greece today, bakers prepare not only hot cross buns but also loaves of Easter breads in a variety of forms, although the most popular is the round loaf that symbolizes eterni-

ty. Greek children often receive gifts of bread from their godparents at Easter.

Did You Know . . .

• Yeast, which makes bread dough rise, is a delicate plant that feeds on sugar and must be grown at a temperature of 70 to 80 degrees Fahrenheit. But yeast also can be made from hops, potatoes, wheat bran, and grains (barley, corn, and rye).

• For centuries in England, the "plowman's lunch" was associated with farm laborers who ate a midday meal of bread, cheese, pickled onions, and beer. Today, this is a popular lunch served in British pubs.

• Since ancient times, bread has been a symbol for life and social customs. It may symbolize the earth, sun, and water, all of which help bring forth grain from the fields and are essential for maintaining life. When there is little bread available, it symbolizes survival; when bread is shared, it symbolizes friendship; and when it is blessed, it symbolizes the presence of the divine.

• In the past, it was common for people to place bread on a dead person's coffin, then eat the bread as a way to consume the person's "sin."

• The term *baker's dozen* dates from the twelfth or thirteenth century. European bakers of that era were nailed by the ears to the doorstop of their bakeries if they sold loaves of bread that were lightweight—contained many large air pockets. To protect themselves from these penalties, they followed the practice of giving out an extra loaf of bread with every dozen loaves distributed to shop or store owners. A storekeeper then sliced off a portion of the thirteenth loaf, adding it to a full loaf to ensure that a customer received full measure.

• No one knows exactly who created the buttery croissant or when it came about, but the roll appears to have international origins. In the late 1600s, the Turks invaded the city of Vienna (Austria), but they were driven out. To celebrate their victory, Viennese bakers made crescent-shaped pastries patterned after the crescent moon emblem on the Turkish flag. By eating the crescent roll, the Viennese could show they had "swallowed up" their enemies. Eventually, Marie Antoinette, an Austrian princess who became queen of France in the 1700s, introduced the roll to French bakers. They created their own version with layers of thin dough, calling it a *croissant,* and this light, flaky roll became a favorite throughout much of Europe. When Americans tasted the croissant, they too declared it a winner, and today the roll is one of the most popular breads in the United States.[3]

CHAPTER 3

A Pinch of Salt, a Sprinkle of Herbs

C AUTION: READ THESE STORIES *cum grano salis!* This Latin phrase, once commonly used, suggests that just as some foods taste better with grains of salt, so some stories are better heard or read with a bit of skepticism.

THE "MAGIC" MINERAL

If you accidentally knock over the saltshaker or spill salt while preparing food, watch out! That could mean

bad luck, unless you quickly throw a pinch of salt over your left shoulder to neutralize any possible misfortune. This superstition has been practiced worldwide for centuries.

Another long-held belief about this natural mineral is that a pinch of salt on a bird's tail works magic: it allows you to catch the bird. Of course, if a winged creature allows you to get that close, you *should* be able to capture it!

Both good and bad omens have been linked to salt. If you had lived in ancient Greece, you likely would have greeted a stranger with a pinch of salt, dropping it into the palm of the person's right hand. Greeks also thought that a pinch of salt dropped into a guest's palm guaranteed that no misfortune would befall him or her while visiting.

In many European countries, salt placed before guests at the table meant a promise of goodwill or the best of luck. But if two people handled the saltshaker at the same time, that could result in a quarrel. It was also bad luck to pass the salt to another person at the table. An old saying in England and the United States cautions: "Pass me salt, pass me sorrow." And if a salt container fell over and spilled toward someone, that, too, was considered unlucky.

Nevertheless, in days past, people also used salt to ward off evil. Greeks and Romans offered their goddesses salt to protect their newborn children, placing a pinch of salt on the baby's tongue. People carried salt in their pockets to entice good fortune when business was conducted and during ceremonies surrounding

events such as births and weddings.

Some eastern Europeans used to sprinkle salt on the doorstep of their new home. Today, some Europeans as well as some Americans still believe that salt should be the first thing brought into a new home to ensure good fortune.

A common practice in Ireland and Scotland was to sprinkle about three handfuls of salt on a dead person in order to purify the corpse. Hawaiians who follow traditional practices say you should sprinkle salt on yourself when you return from a funeral to ensure that evil spirits who might be hovering about the dead won't follow you into your home.

Salt is a valuable commodity because it can preserve or enhance the taste of many foods. But it was not abundant during ancient times, so working people often received an allotment of salt as pay for their labor. As a result, if someone said you were "worth your salt," that meant your work was highly valued and you were held in high esteem.

A man who is worth his salt.

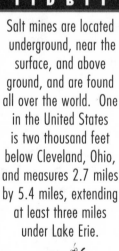

TIDBIT

Salt mines are located underground, near the surface, and above ground, and are found all over the world. One in the United States is two thousand feet below Cleveland, Ohio, and measures 2.7 miles by 5.4 miles, extending at least three miles under Lake Erie.

WELCOME TO
CLEVELAND
HOME OF AN EXTREMELY
LARGE SALT MINE.

Because of the importance of salt, a huge saltcellar, or container, sat on the table of nobility, dividing people at the table according to their rank. Those of the highest class sat above the salt, or near the head of the table, while lower-class guests and servants were seated "below the salt."

Today, some people believe that the saltshaker should be full on New Year's Day in order to ensure prosperity throughout the year. Others say that you should never lend or borrow salt (or pepper either) because that will destroy a friendship. To prevent such bad luck, just don't pay back what you borrowed. Mexican lore says that a household should never run out of salt; otherwise the family could suffer misfortune.

HERBAL CUSTOMS

Herbs have long been used for medicinal purposes, brewed in teas as a sedative or a stimulant, and served as garnishes or as flavor enhancements for foods. Herbal compounds—both fresh and dried—for cooking and teas are widely popular today. In fact, herbs are being analyzed by scientists around the world for components that could be used in the manufacture of drugs to cure a variety of diseases from AIDS to cancer. But besides these practical purposes, herbs have been seen as mysterious plants and have been used in many symbolic rituals.

The shiny green leaves of the bay laurel tree or shrub, for example, have a rich history as symbols of glory and honor. During the early Olympic Games, a crown of bay leaves would adorn a winner's head. Laurel leaves and twigs have been widely used as love charms, and some people say that laurel leaves on your pillow at night could bring you dreams of love.

One old superstition declares that bay leaves thrown on a fire must crackle to bring good luck; if they burn without a sound, too bad. That may be an unlucky sign. Today, a belief still persists that a bay leaf found in a plate of stew, a bowl of soup, or in a casserole serving is a sign of good fortune.

Countless other herbs have been imbued with symbolic and magical qualities. Basil, for example, is reported to have a great variety of magical capabilities, from enhancing love to protecting against evil spells. In some parts of the United States today, home gardeners say that if you want to ensure good luck, plant basil on each side of your doorstep. On the other hand, basil was feared by Europeans of the Middle Ages, because they believed the herb would produce deadly scorpions, although no one seemed to know exactly how that would happen.

Another herb, parsley, was once thought to be sacred, and therefore ancient Greeks refused to eat it or use it for a garnish. But Romans thought it a tasty accent to food. Early Greeks and Romans also used parsley to decorate tombs since the herb was supposed to aid in resurrection. Yet some people today think it is unlucky to put parsley plants in a garden or to transplant parsley from one place to another. "Transplant parsley, transplant death" is the old saying. But it's okay to sow parsley seed and let it grow naturally. If you do grow parsley from seed, however, don't give away any of the plants. That's giving away your luck!

Etruscans who lived in an area that is now part of Italy believed that still another herb, rue, helped ward off disease if a sprig was worn as an amulet. Italians later used rue as a protection against the evil eye. Rue leaves, walnuts, figs, and a pinch of salt were used to make a folk medicine antidote for poison. The British, too, believed that rue would safeguard them from the plague and other serious diseases. Some Turks have carried on the belief that rue has protective powers, and to ensure good fortune, they will carry the plant wherever they travel at home and abroad—if allowed by law to carry it across national borders.

DID YOU KNOW . . .

- *Botanicas* are places that combine magic rituals with some commonsense advice about health remedies, including the use of herbs for healing. Botanica healers have been called the doctors, druggists, psychologists, and priests of the poor, because herbal medicines are relatively inexpensive. Many herbs, in fact, can be gathered in the wild.

• Bouquets made of herbs were used in Europe to ward off disease in medieval times. Called tussie-mussies, or nosegays, they are still displayed in English courts of law.

Tussie-Mussie

CHAPTER 4

MAGICAL FRUITS, SEEDS, AND NUTS

Try This Fruit-and-Nuts Tongue Twister

Peter Piper picked a peck of prickly pears, a pound of puny peaches, and a pail of paltry peanuts.
Did Peter Piper pick a peck of prickly peaches, pound of puny peanuts, and pail of paltry pears?
Or perhaps Peter Piper picked a peck of prickly peanuts, pound of puny pears, and pail of paltry peaches?
If Peter Piper picked a peck, pound, and pail of produce, I'm perplexed. Where's the peck, pound, and pail of produce Peter Piper picked?

FROM APPLE LORE TO WATERMELON legends, stories about the magic of eating various fruits abound. The old saying "An apple a day keeps the doctor away" sprouted from folklore, but it is partially based on fact, too. An apple in your daily diet certainly does not guarantee good health for life, but it's a food that supplies Vitamin C, carotene, potassium, boron, and fiber. Apples even serve as a partial cleaner for your teeth. If, for example, you've eaten an apple after devouring a peanut butter sandwich, you know that chewing an apple clears away the sticky goo. The apple cannot take the place of a toothbrush, but it helps.

Apple superstitions are numerous. In the Garden of Eden story, the apple (which could have been a pomegranate or an apricot, since apples were unknown in biblical lands) was a forbidden fruit. Adam was banished from paradise because

he ate the fruit that Eve offered him. Perhaps this story prompted an old belief that before eating an apple, one should rub it to remove any evil spirits that might be inside. (Of course, you *could* be rubbing it to remove any dirt, too.)

One old superstition declares that rubbing an apple on a baby's tongue will ensure that the child has a good singing voice. Another insists that dropping a snake in a barrel of apple cider will make the cider sweet.

You can find your "true love" with apples and apple seeds. Give an apple the name of a person, split the apple in half, and the named person magically experiences love for you. Another way to determine who's in love with you is to put apple seeds in a pan and name each one of them. Then place the pan on a hot stove; the first seed to pop names your "true love."

Variations of this belief have carried over to the common Halloween game of bobbing for apples. Apples floating in a washtub full of water may be named. Wearing a blindfold, contestants try to grab an apple with their teeth. The name of the "captured" apple foretells the "bobber's" future spouse.

Another type of apple divination is to carefully pare an apple, making sure that the peeling stays in one unbroken curly piece. Then throw the peeling over your left shoulder or over your head. When it lands, you will see the shape of a letter, which stands for the first name of your true love. It might help to use

an old chant, popular in the 1800s, that goes like this:

> **St. Simon and St. Jude,**
> **On you I intrude;**
> **By this paring I hold to discover,**
> **Without any delay,**
> **To tell me this day,**
> **The first letter of my own**
>   **true lover.**[4]

Or you could use a simplified version of the chant: "Apple peel, apple peel, twist then rest/Show me the one that I'll love best."

Apricots, bananas, grapes, and peaches are among many other fruits thought to be "love bearers," and fruits with multiple seeds are commonly linked with fertility and prosperity. The pomegranate certainly fits those categories. In fact, it is considered one of the luckiest fruits in American folklore. Your money may even multiply if you rub your coins and bills with pomegranate seeds.

Figs have lots of seeds, too, but they have not always been considered lucky. In the Mediterranean, these fruits were at times thought to be harbingers of evil, although at other times they were venerated as a life-giving force.

The ancient Hebrews believed that figs could cure boils, and the

THE MAGIC BANANA

HUNDREDS OF YEARS ago, after the Polynesians migrated throughout the islands of the Pacific and settled in Hawaii, they created a legend about a magic banana. The story is told to this day. It begins with Kukali, the son of a priest, who had numerous magical powers and received a magic banana from his father. Kukali was told to maintain control over the fruit at all times and to carefully preserve the skin when eating from the banana so that he would always have a food supply.

Kukali loved adventure and traveled to distant islands, tramping through forests and climbing mountains. The only food he carried was the magic banana. When he got hungry, he ate the banana but always folded the skin together. Then, within a short time, the banana appeared again. He repeated this process over and over and always kept a close watch on the banana skin. As a result he was never without food.

During his adventures, Kukali suffered some terrible misfortunes. Once he was captured by a great bird-god that ate humans. While he was imprisoned, Kukali was able to protect and save some of his fellow prisoners, feeding them from his magic banana. In time, he and other prisoners were able to escape and destroy the bird.

But the bird-god's sister learned of her brother's death and tried to find ways to overcome Kukali's power. One method was to tempt Kukali to eat ripe fruit, which was poisoned. But Kukali continued to eat only from his magic banana, astounding everyone around him because this wizard, as he was called, ate ripe fruit but survived! After many trials and tribulations, Kukali convinced everyone that he was the most powerful wizard around, and he eventually married the bird-god's sister and returned to Hawaii.[5]

prophet Isaiah ordered "a cake of figs" to "lay on the boil" of King Hezekiah "so that he may recover."[6] For centuries in India, the fig tree has been considered sacred, with its roots in heaven and branches extending down to earth. In the past, the juice or "milk" of figs was used as a remedy for toothache, and the bark of the fig tree was ground to make a medicine that was supposed to help a person control diabetes.

Some fruits bring bad luck for sure, it's been said. Anyone who carelessly throws away a banana skin

> **TIDBIT**
>
> In the botanical world, the banana plant is classified as an herb, not a fruit tree, and the plant technically produces berries—bananas.

may suffer a painful death, some people believe. Even if such a tragedy were averted, it's best to watch where you throw a banana peel since you or someone else could slip on it and take a painful fall. In Hawaii, some folks may advise you not to take a banana on a fishing boat; if you do, you won't have any luck catching fish![7]

Another bit of folk wisdom from Hawaii says that a watermelon rolled out the front door of a deceased person's home helps that person's spirit reach heaven. In other parts of the United States, watermelons may not

have spiritual links to heaven, but they are considered good antidotes for many ailments—from fever to smallpox. Some elderly folks in the South advise children not to swallow watermelon seeds, because watermelons might grow out of their ears! One way to avoid such a catastrophe, according to superstitious belief, is to take part in a seed-spitting contest.

To those who celebrate the Chinese New Year, which is based on a lunar calendar and begins with a new moon sometime between late January and February, the luckiest fruits are oranges and tangerines. Why? Because these fruits have a reddish-orange color, and red is a Chinese symbol of good luck.

Oranges also have symbolized good fortune in many other cultures. Some Americans of Italian descent, for example, have followed the practice of eating an orange slice for good luck on Christmas Eve. In many parts of the world, the blossoms of orange trees and their evergreen branches have been associated with long-lasting love and fertility, and brides have worn orange blossom wreaths as a part of the bridal headdress to ensure a happy marriage and many children. That custom was practiced in some parts of the United States until about the 1920s, but it is not common today.

It's long been an American practice to put an orange in a Christmas stocking, although the custom is sometimes supplanted by stuffing stockings with a variety of prepackaged, commercial items from candy to rings to small toys. Stuffing stockings with food gifts has been a long-standing European Christmas ritual, and some historians believe it stemmed from a practice that had nothing to do with Christianity or the birth of Christ. Instead, it may have originated in ancient times when people offered containers of food to the gods that were thought to be responsible for providing a good harvest.

DID YOU KNOW . . .

• In many different cultures over the ages, a fruit tree has been considered a "tree of life." The Celts, for example, honor the apple tree. In China the peach tree is a life giver. And in many parts of the Mediterranean the fig tree is designated the tree of life.

• In Norway, it's common for children to make a hole in the top of an orange large enough to get a lump of sugar inside and then

suck out the juice—a practice that many Americans have copied.

• Tomatoes were once called "love apples" in Europe because it was believed that these fruits increased sexual passion and cured sterility. In North America, on the other hand, the tomato was considered a poisonous fruit. (It's actually a berry.) Eventually the tomato was labeled a vegetable by order of the U.S. Supreme Court, settling a court case in 1893 over tariffs on fruits and vegetables.

• Since colonial times, the pineapple has been a symbol of hospitality, and a pineap-

TIDBIT

Half of the peanuts grown in the United States are ground up for peanut butter. Americans consume 800 million pounds of this spread each year—that averages more than three pounds per person.

ple sign over the entrance to a motel or hotel means "welcome." The custom stems from the days when ship captains returned home with cargo and put a pineapple outside to signal that neighbors and friends should stop by and share in the bounty.

• Peanuts are not actually nuts. Rather, they are a type of legume and were once called ground-nuts or ground-peas, because they begin their growth underground and the plant grows close to the earth, producing pods and "nuts" that look like peas in a pod.

Another fruit steeped in superstition is the cherry.

FRUITFUL PHRASES

A NUMBER OF COMMON sayings and expressions in the English language allude to various fruits, particularly the powerful apple. Translations are at right.

1. An apple knocker
2. The apple of my eye
3. In apple-pie order
4. They're apple polishing
5. The Big Apple
6. A rotten apple
7. They've gone bananas
8. The top banana
9. It's the berries
10. A fruitcake
11. The grapefruit league
12. It's a lemon
13. He's a melon-belly
14. It's not worth a fig
15. It's peachy-keen (or peachy)
16. A rhubarb
17. Sour grapes
18. She's swallowed a watermelon seed

TRANSLATIONS:

(1) a country person, someone who knocks fruit from an apple tree; (2) a favorite/loved/admired person; (3) neatly arranged; (4) trying to gain favor; (5) New York City; (6) unsavory person; (7) gone crazy, gotten hysterical; (8) highest-ranking person; (9) the best; (10) an eccentric or insane person; (11) major league baseball teams in competition during spring training in citrus growing areas; (12) a defective car or other unsatisfactory product; (13) a man with a large, protruding abdomen; (14) worthless; (15) wonderful; (16) a heated argument; (17) disparagement of something that is especially wanted but unattainable; (18) description of a pregnant woman.

The Apple of my Eye   Gone Bananas

Sour Grapes

Maybe you've heard an old folk saying common in the United States: "Swallow a cherry pit, and a tree will grow in your stomach." If it were true, some folks would be in big trouble. There are those who claim to get a pit every time they eat cherry pie or cobbler. That bit of bad luck multiplied over a lifetime could produce an orchard!

An old superstition contends that if an un-married man can shoot a cherry seed with his thumb and index finger toward the ceiling and make a hit on his first try, he's bound to marry soon. What about an unmarried woman? She should count a plateful of cherry seeds by pointing to each seed and chanting "this year" with the first, "next year" with the sec-ond, and "sometime" and "never" with the third and fourth, repeating the process until she reaches the last cherry seed, which marks her fate.

Unlike cherry seeds, the pits of olives are not necessarily good or bad luck charms. But olive oil has been considered magical, protecting against drunkenness and helping to

TIDBIT

Long before colonial times, Native Americans ground nuts—acorns, chestnuts, hazelnuts, hickory nuts, walnuts, and others—into meal used to make bread or to thicken soups and stews. Sometimes the meal was mixed with water to make a "milk," or nuts were boiled to extract the oil for use as a spread on bread.

relieve stress if consumed. To anoint with olive oil has also been part of religious purification ceremonies, and an olive branch has long sym-bolized peace.

NUTTY NONSENSE

If you like to carry an amulet for luck, you might want to consider a double walnut, a chestnut, or even a peach stone—a seed that looks very much like a nut. These and many other nuts and seeds have been used for ages as good luck charms, worn on neck-laces, carried in pockets, or just kept in a safe place.

Like apples and apple seeds, nuts were commonly used in seventeenth-, eighteenth-, and nineteenth-century Europe as love charms, and the prac-tice carried over to colonial America. Young people would name unshelled nuts, giving one a boy's name, an-other a girl's name, and so on. Then they'd be thrown in a fire to deter-mine their fate. A cracking shell or a nut that jumped signified an unde-pendable lover. But a burst of flame was the sign of a true love.

dow shades. People used to tie acorns to strings or make various types of coverings for acorn pulls. Acorns were also sewn into jackets or other clothing as protection from thunder and lightning.

Because of the shape and appearance of the walnut, people once believed this nut could cure diseases of the brain. Walnuts and hazelnuts also guaranteed a long life and fertility. Sometimes these nuts were scattered about before a wedding, or they were given to couples when they married in order to ensure they would have many children.

The chestnut, or "buckeye," also symbolized fertility. These nuts supposedly signified long life as well,

Throughout recorded history, the oak tree has been known as the king of trees, so the acorns they produce have been considered powerful charms. They were thought to safeguard a home from storms, for instance, if they were placed on windowsills or used as pulls on win-

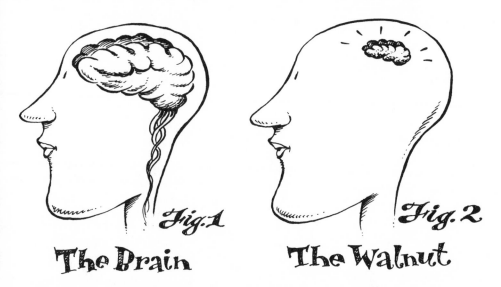

Fig. 1
The Brain

Fig. 2
The Walnut

a belief that probably originated in China and other parts of Asia where the chestnut tree has grown since remote times and is long-lived. On the other hand, the fruits of this tree have a connection with death, too; in many parts of the world, chestnuts are left as offerings to assist the deceased on their journey to the spirit world.

In American folklore, chestnuts are thought to have special powers as curatives. People often carried chestnuts in their pockets to ward off or relieve the pain of arthritis and rheumatism. But if the shells of the chestnuts were cracked, their "magic" wouldn't work. So they had to be replaced with new chestnuts, their shells fully intact.

CHAPTER 5

FROM HOPPIN' JOHN TO POPEYE'S "POWER" VEGGIE

Never tell a secret in a cornfield —
There are too many ears around

TO START EACH NEW YEAR WITH GOOD luck your motto might be "eat your vegetables." But certain vegetables are considered particularly lucky. Many North Americans follow the German tradition of eating sauerkraut on New Year's Day, bringing wealth, good health, and other good fortune to their home.

Cabbage and black-eyed peas cooked with pork or ham are a good luck combination in many southern U.S. homes. Some people cook cabbage or peas with a dime or other silver to make sure there will be plenty of food and money during the year. Collard greens also are eaten to ensure that money will be plentiful in the coming year. Hoppin' John, a special dish made with rice and peas, is a traditional New Year's dish in the South. Almost every cook who prepares this harbinger of good fortune creates her or his own version, but basically the recipe is as follows:

TIDBIT

People have been growing lettuce for more than 2,500 years, and Americans eat about 8,500 tons of fresh lettuce daily.

HOPPIN' JOHN
A GOOD LUCK RECIPE

1 pound dried black-eyed peas or field peas

1/2 to 3/4 pound
salt pork or ham hocks

1 green pepper, chopped

1 onion, chopped

1 bay leaf

salt and pepper to taste

steamed rice

Rinse and then soak the peas overnight. Place salt pork or ham hocks in 1 1/2 quarts of water and bring to boil. Drain the peas and add to the boiling ham hocks. Add chopped green pepper and onion, bay leaf, and salt and pepper. Cover and simmer for about one hour or until peas are tender. Cook 2 to 2 1/2 cups of white rice. When peas are done and only a small amount of water remains, add the cooked rice and season with cayenne pepper and/or Cajun spices. Serve with onion slices, hot sauce, cornbread, and greens.

LUCKY VEGGIES YEAR 'ROUND

Beyond heralding luck for the New Year, certain vegetables supposedly work their magic all year long. Artichokes, for example, are supposed to provide protective power anytime they are eaten. Consuming asparagus enhances sexual desire.

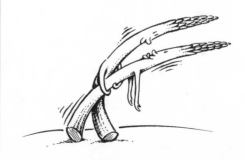

Any young woman who finds nine peas in a pod is in for a lucky surprise: The next single young man to come to her home will become her husband, or so the British have long believed.

Beans—both the shelled kind (like limas and kidney beans) and those in the pod (such as string beans)—are thought to be especially lucky and are offered to gods and celebrated in festivals. Societies around the world have used beans in connection with ceremonies for the dead, scattering beans throughout a home to drive out demons. Spitting beans was also considered a magical way to keep witches and ghosts away.

Cabbage is also considered a good luck food. The Irish, for example, wrap cabbage leaves around a meat-and-vegetable combination to create a symbolic dish of plenty for St. Patrick's Day and a lucky dish for other times of the year. A Hungarian good luck dish is stuffed cabbage strudel made with shredded cabbage sautéed with onion, pepper, caraway seeds, sugar, and cinnamon, layered in phyllo leaves, and baked.

Another lucky vegetable is the tomato, although the tomato is not technically a vegetable—it's the berry of a fruit plant. A large red tomato on the windowsill guards

MAGIC BEANS

THE OLD ENGLISH FOLKtale "Jack and the Beanstalk," which has been told with many variations, focuses on the magical properties of beans. As you may recall, Jack's mother sent him to market to sell their cow so they would have some money. But Jack traded the cow for five magic beans. His mother was so angry about what she considered an absurd transaction that she threw the beans out the window. But the next morning, beside the house, was a gigantic beanstalk reaching to the sky. Jack climbed the beanstalk and at the top found a road leading to the home of a rich giant, whose main occupation was counting his golden eggs while chanting in deep, ominous tones "Fe, fi, fo, fum!" and threatening to devour any Englishman in sight.

Jack was able to steal a bag of gold on his first visit. On a second climb up the beanstalk, he captured the goose that laid the golden eggs. And the third time, he whisked away the giant's magic harp. The giant chased Jack, and the crafty boy slid down the beanstalk with the giant close behind. But Jack chopped the beanstalk down, bringing the giant crashing to earth. Of course, that was the end of the giant, and Jack and his mother lived happily ever after in wealth and style.

produce a good harvest. In the United States today, Native American corn festivals are modern versions of paying homage to the natural forces that help produce this all-purpose food.

Native Americans and other corn growers also have passed on some

against evil spirits, say some believers. If a real tomato isn't available, a pincushion shaped like a tomato will do the trick. The pincushion reportedly came about because people didn't ever want to be without something at least resembling the lucky tomato.

THE POWER OF CORN

For centuries, many Native Americans have grown numerous varieties of corn in colors ranging from yellow to red to blue, and they have used almost every part of the corn plant either for food or for medicinal or household purposes. Within this culture, there is a long-held belief that Corn Gods, Corn Mothers, and Corn Priests watch over the corn crops. Indeed, corn plants and corn are so important that they are considered sacred, and incantations, songs, and rituals have long been performed to help corn grow and

superstitions about corn. They say finding a red ear of corn is a sign of good luck. Corn may also guard infants. If an ear of corn is placed alongside a newborn, no evil spirit can capture the child's soul.

Along with superstitions, there are numerous legends and tall tales about corn. One from Nebraska tells about the origin of the popcorn ball, which apparently created itself. It seems that during a hot, rainy summer in the 1800s, a Nebraska farmer grew sugarcane on a hillside and corn in the valley below. Weather conditions, as is often true in the Midwest, varied from one field to the other. Rain clouds let loose over the cane fields while rays from the hot sun blistered the corn. It got so hot, in fact, that the corn began to pop.

At the same time, the rain over the cane field washed sugar from the stalks, sending the syrupy stuff down the hill over the popped corn and rolling it into huge balls. The farmer wasn't able to share the popcorn balls with his family or neighbors, however, because a great horde of grasshoppers arrived, consuming every popcorn ball in sight—at least that's what he told everyone who was salivating for one of the giant treats![8]

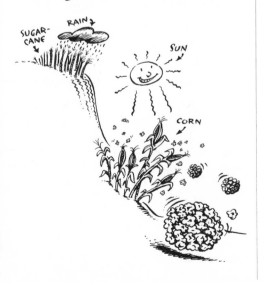

A LANTERN NAMED FOR A TRICKSTER

ONE VEGETABLE LONG associated with superstitious practices is the pumpkin, hollowed out and carved like a grotesque mask or face and lit by a candle inside. Such a lantern was named for a legendary will-o'-the-wisp: a misleading Irish character named Jack. According to the story, Jack was condemned to wander the earth because he was a trickster and was not accepted in either Heaven or Hell. Some of the first jack-o'-lanterns were made from potatoes, turnips, or other vegetables that could be carved to hold a lighted candle.

Jack-o'-lanterns, the superstitious say, are meant to light the way for travelers who, if they're not careful, could be fooled by a goblin or sprite intent on leading the unwary into a swamp or other dangerous place. These ghosts and goblins supposedly appear on All Hallow's Eve—Halloween. Today, the Halloween celebration includes pumpkins or manufactured plastic jack-o'-lanterns and people dressed in costumes, keeping the day-of-the-dead alive—certainly a misnomer of sorts.

WART REMOVERS AND OTHER VEGGIE "CURES"

A number of vegetables are supposed to be cures for a great variety of ailments. Corn, for example, can cure warts, say the superstitious. How? Well, you could bury a bag of corn and wait for the kernels to decompose. By then, your warts should be gone. Some people suggest rubbing a wart with an ear of corn to remove the unwanted growth. Or you could try a more elaborate ritual after rubbing the wart: Bore a hole in a tree trunk, put the corn inside, and plug up the hole! In Texas they say you should stick a pin or needle in a wart, then when it bleeds pull it out and stick it

TIDBIT

Most of the large variety of pumpkins grown in the United States are too stringy to eat, and about 99 percent are sold to make jack-o'-lanterns for Halloween celebrations.

Not Good Enough For Pie

into a kernel of corn, bury the kernel in the earth, and as the corn begins to grow, your wart will disappear.

Peas and beans are supposed to be good wart removers, too. So is eggplant, according to Hawaiian belief. You have to rub this vegetable on the wart and then bury the eggplant. But if you are feeling rather mean, throw the eggplant into the street. Then someone else can be inflicted with your wart.

Do you want a cure for a sore throat? Cabbage leaves, it is said, will do the trick. But don't eat the leaves; tie them around your neck!

Another superstition about cabbage decrees that whoever eats this vegetable while drinking alcoholic beverages will not get drunk. Why not? According to the "logic" of magic, the grapevine does not grow where the cabbage plant lives, but how that prevents drunkenness is anyone's guess.

Potatoes provide some special "cures." After boiling potatoes with their skins on, you can place them on your *feet* to relieve a cold in the

The Toe Potato Cure

head, so it's said. If you eat potato peelings (although please not the same ones that were on your feet!), you can grow hair on your chest—assuming that's where you want it. Some people believe that you should carry a potato in your pocket to prevent rheumatism. Scrapings from a raw potato are supposed to heal burns and frostbite. According to the Irish, water from boiled potatoes is similar to a good rubbing alcohol; use it for aches and sprains and even to ease the pain of broken bones.

In England centuries ago, people believed that lettuce could prevent or alleviate lung disease. Why? The lettuce leaf is shaped like the human lung, so people thought it must have been de-

signed to "cure" that part of the body. It was also common to eat a head of lettuce to prevent seasickness on a voyage.

The magical properties of pungent garlic and its close relative, the eye-stinging onion, have been touted for centuries. Ancient Egyptians believed that the onion represented eternity and guarded against evil and diseases like the plague. In fact, throughout the ages, people worldwide have believed in the magical power of onions and garlic to ward off infection and to heal a great variety of ailments from earache and nosebleed to venomous snake and insect bites.

If you want to get rid of a cold, superstition

> **T I D B I T**
>
> In some countries, *corn* means grain—almost any type of grain, such as wheat or rye.

says you should hang an onion from a string or cord and give the onion a knock each time you pass. Carry an onion in your pocket to ward off colds and seizures. To stop a nosebleed, place onions on the back of your neck.

SNIFFLE

How do you get rid of a fever? Some people say you should apply mashed onions as a compress to several parts of your body: the stomach, armpits, bottoms of your feet, and in the palms of your hands. But this remedy may also drive away your friends and relatives along with your fever!

Some superstitious folks may tell you to cut an onion in half and put it on a shelf or windowsill and diseases will be absorbed by this vegetable. On the other hand, some believe that a cut onion in the home is bad luck, and they immediately throw away any unused portion.

Great magical feats have been attributed to garlic. Many centuries ago, garlic was thought to be godlike and was worshiped. This supernatural vegetable could not only cure diseases and prevent aches and pains but also help a person develop courage and many other beneficial characteristics.

KEEPS AWAY VAMPIRES, FLEAS, COLDS, AND UNWANTED ADVANCES.

Garlic superstitions have been the most prevalent in Mediterranean countries, where people have long worn cloves of garlic around the neck as a protective charm against the evil eye, a look capable of inflicting harm. Some people in the United States follow the practice as well. Hanging strings of garlic over a doorway to a home was—and still is in many places—thought to be a way to prevent evil spirits from entering. Garlic hung over a fireplace mantel is supposed to bring good luck as well as ward off diseases.

THE "POWER" VEGETABLE

"I'm Popeye the Sailor Man,
I'm Popeye the Sailor Man . . ."

Most Americans are familiar with this tune—the trademark of the cartoon character Popeye, created in 1930. On film, Popeye has sung about and dramatized the magical properties of spinach, and generations of Americans have watched Popeye down a can of the leafy, green vegetable and gain superhuman strength to save his girlfriend, Olive Oyl, and others from every kind of disaster imaginable.

Long before Popeye came on the scene, people around the world touted the near-miraculous benefits of eating spinach. Ages ago, some people thought spinach was lifesaving. Others swore it had a soothing effect when eaten, or that the vegetable could generate feelings of romance.

In the more recent past, nutritionists have debunked myths about the benefits of spinach. Although the vegetable certainly provides vitamins and minerals that the human body needs, it is not a major "power" source. Yet food experts may not convince Popeye fans, who can hardly forget the sailor man's boast: *"I'm strong to the finish, 'cause I eat me spinach. I'm Popeye the Sailor Man!"*

DID YOU KNOW . . .

- The "World's Only Corn Palace," as it's advertised across the United States, stands in Mitchell, South Dakota, just off Interstate 90. A monument to the nation's "king crop," the building is covered with tens of thousands of cobs of corn in colors ranging from pink to orange-yellow to black. The corncobs are arranged in designs and murals, which are changed each year to fit a particular theme. Local people spend weeks after the harvest pounding the corncobs in place.

- Only about 1 percent of the corn grown in the United States is for direct human consumption. But corn is an essential feed for the millions of animals that Americans eat, and corn-based products are found in many processed foods as well as nonfood items. Check out labels of foods on grocery shelves or at home, and you'll find ingredients ranging from corn syrup to corn oil and cornstarch. Corn products also are used to manufacture lipstick, toothpaste, glue, embalming fluid, paper products, ethanol (fuel), explosives, and countless other items.

- For years, parents have urged their children to eat potato skins because the outer covering was considered the most nutritious part of the vegetable. But that

theory has been challenged. Some nutritionists now say that the potato skin contains no more nutrients than the inside pulp and that a toxin called solanine in the skin could be harmful. Yet other researchers say that the toxin in small concentrations is harmless and that only potatoes exposed to light for long periods or to extreme temperatures develop large amounts of the poison.

• By the 1600s, the Incas were growing three thousand different types of potatoes in the Andes region of South America. Today, the International Potato Institute located in the region studies and categorizes about ten thousand varieties of potatoes that have been cultivated or found in the wild of the Andes Mountains. The potatoes range in color from white and yellow to green to blue and black.

CRYING OVER MILK, CHANTING FOR BUTTER, AND "DYING" FOR YOGURT

WAAAAA!

"THERE'S NO USE CRYING OVER spilled milk" is a bit of sage advice that has been repeated often since about the mid-1800s. Even though it was considered a great

loss—and bad luck—to spill milk, the saying points out that once something unfortunate happens,

it's best to try to go on without great lament.

Through the ages, milk has been

the first food for most newborns. Infants usually received mother's milk, so it's not surprising that this food has been considered a divine gift and has been surrounded by magical practices and superstitions. In Sri Lanka, for example, a tiny bit of gold mixed with mother's milk was placed on a newborn's tongue to ensure good fortune. An eastern European mother would never offer her left breast when feeding her child for the first time, since that would create a left-handed child.

Women in many countries have believed that there are auspicious times for weaning a child from breast-feeding. In Poland, it was a common belief that a mother should wean her child when the moon was full in order to make sure that her child would have a round, beautiful face. Another fortunate time to stop breast-feeding was when trees sprouted and blossomed, ensuring that the child would forever be young. But a mother would not wean her child while leaves were falling because that could lead to early baldness for the child. And weaning did not take place "when birds were flying away for the winter, for fear the child

would grow up to be wild and take to the forest and woods," according to Polish folklore.[9]

Among some Asian, African, Mediterranean, Native American, and a few other groups, children are not usually given milk after they are weaned, because as they grow older they do not have the enzyme needed to digest milk from animal sources. Without the enzyme, drinking milk causes intestinal problems, so beliefs have developed and persisted about the evils of this food. But for many groups worldwide, milk and milk products have been part of the diet for centuries, and superstitions and magical practices have focused on protecting the milk supply and products made from milk, such as butter, cheese, and yogurt.

Offerings of milk and milk products were presented to gods and goddesses. Sometimes melted butter or yogurt (made from fermented milk) was poured over statues of deities. In India, *ghee*, or clarified butter—a liquid butter with the fat removed—was the divine food and is still used by Hindus in religious ceremonies.

Until just a few decades ago, many farmers believed they had to guard against

TIDBIT

In some countries, people once spread butter on their bodies to protect themselves from bugs and to keep warm.

various practices that might put a curse on their milk cows and make them unable to produce milk. Don't stir a glass of milk with a fork, a farmer might tell you, as that will make the cow go dry. It was also a bad omen to let milk boil over the side of a pan. To counteract that type of accident, a person had to throw salt on the fire.

Besides being an important part of the diet for many people, milk is thought to prevent drunkenness if consumed before a night of boozing. This notion is closely related to an ancient Roman belief that became part of American folklore as well: One should take a dose of olive or mineral oil before heavy drinking. It was believed that the oil coated the stomach and prevented alcohol

from being absorbed. Milk is supposed to do the same thing. However, stomach acids begin to work almost at once on any food in the stomach, quickly changing it into a substance other than milk, oil, or whatever is introduced.

Another old belief claims that milk can help forecast the weather. How? First you'd have to fill a jar nearly full of water, then pour in a little milk. If the mixture cleared up quickly, a mild winter would be ahead. But if the mixture stayed cloudy for quite a while, you could expect a cold, wet winter.

CHANTING FOR BUTTER

Farmers thought butter appeared magically from the fatty part of milk—the cream—and that witches could prevent the butter from forming when the milk was churned to separate the cream from the milk. To guard against this sorcery, people often put salt in a churn, or took a horseshoe hot from the fire and let it sizzle briefly in the milk. Sometimes they just tied a lucky charm to the butter churn itself.

Magical or semireligious chants were also a part of butter making. It was common, while operating a butter churn, to repeat incantations like this:

Come, butter, come,
Come, butter, come,
Peter stands at the gate
Waiting for a buttered cake,
Come, butter, come.

Some Americans will tell you that the buttermilk left after cream turns to butter is an excellent antidote for a freckled face. If you don't like freckles, just wash in buttermilk, and the freckles will disappear—or at least they'll be covered with buttery splotches!

"THE MILK OF ETERNAL LIFE"

Yogurt, which is made from sour or fermented milk, is another dairy product that has been used for the skin since ancient times. Early Persian women, for example, used yogurt as a complexion cream and were convinced that it would remove facial lines and wrinkles, clear up blemishes and blotchy skin, and make their faces more youthful looking. Even today, some women use yogurt for a beauty mask, dabbing it on, letting it dry for hours or overnight, then rinsing it off. Some say this preparation is as effec-tive as any commercial beauty mask.

No one knows whether such claims are true; none have been substantiated with scientific studies. But the beliefs about yogurt's power to improve one's appearance and well-being have been around for at least four thousand years!

Great writers and orators of old proclaimed that yogurt could cure myriad health problems and drive evil spirits from the soul. Emperor Francis I, a French ruler of the

TIDBIT

People once thought that thunder curdled milk and helped produce yogurt.

sixteenth century, apparently was pulled from the brink of death by a yogurt remedy, and from then on he called yogurt "the milk of eternal life." Today, people around the world continue to praise yogurt's "magical" benefits, but there still is no proof that it has any more nutritional value than the milk from which it's made.

DID YOU KNOW . . .

• Until the early 1900s, people in Mediterranean countries thought that butter caused leprosy or, at the very least, was a food fit only for barbarians. Instead of butter, people used olive oil as a spread or for cooking. Butter also was used as a remedy for skin injuries like burns and rashes. Some modern folks still use butter for that purpose today, although it's not a medically recommended treatment.

• One oft-repeated legend says that yogurt originated accidentally in the Middle East when a nomad carried a goatskin bag of milk with him as he traveled across the desert on his camel. The desert heat and bacteria inside the bag helped ferment the milk and turn it into a custardlike substance.

• Cow's milk is not the only source for yogurt. Milk from camels, goats, ewes, mares, water buffalo, yaks, and other animals can be clabbered, or curdled, by bacteria (*Lactobacillus bulgaricus* and *Streptococcus lactis*) to make a fermented dairy product. Bulgarians, for example, use milk from water buffalo and goats (high in butterfat) to produce a rich yogurt that is one of the world's best.

CHAPTER 7

BURYING, CRACKING, DECORATING, HIDING, TOSSING, SMASHING, ROLLING— AND SOMETIMES EATING— EGGS

**Humpty Dumpty
sat on a wall,**

Humpty Dumpty had a great fall

LONG BEFORE THIS RIDDLE WAS TOLD and retold, countless rhymes, tales, and myths about the egg were created and passed on in every part of the world. As early people watched various forms of life appear from eggs, they no doubt began to draw conclusions about their own world: The Earth itself must have hatched

This is so *eggsasperating!*

All the king's horses, And all the king's men Couldn't put Humpty together again.

from a gigantic cosmic egg!

Thus the egg was a symbol of the universe and endowed with magical powers that were invoked in numerous superstitious practices and rituals, particularly fertility rites. In many countries, eggs were placed atop the wedding bread or cake to ensure that the newly married couple would have children.

In Europe, the egg was thought to bring life to various crops. When it was time to sow grain, a farmer would take an egg into the field to ensure that the grain would sprout and grow well. Some farmers would throw eggshells onto the ground between rows of grain or vegetables, believing that this would help bring about a good yield. In some cases, farmers buried eggs near fruit trees to increase their harvest.

Some Europeans in times past buried eggs beside rivers or dropped them into wells or streams to appease the jinni, or spirits, that supposedly controlled these water sources. Displeased spirits might make the water dry up. If a child accidentally fell into a stream, the youngster after being rescued had to throw an egg into the water as a sacrifice to the water spirits. Eggs, eggshells, and artificial eggs often were buried along with bodies in graves and tombs, apparently to symbolize rebirth in another world.

> *Break an egg,*
> *Break your leg,*
> *Break three,*
> *Woe to thee;*
> *Break two,*
> *Your love's true.*

This old chant was often recited when people collected eggs, trying to ward off any misfortune that might come about if eggs were broken accidentally. Finding many broken eggs in a henhouse signaled an argument or a lawsuit in the near future. And no hen should have an even number of eggs to hatch—that would bring bad luck. Dreaming about broken eggs was considered bad luck, too. But if you dreamed about many eggs, that would be a sign of good fortune coming your way.

Egg whites were used for forecasting as well. A person had to crack an egg and drop the white into a glass, bowl, or jug of water. Then the egg white formed a shape that supposedly predicted future events. Sometimes the egg-white-and-water mixture was left outdoors or placed on a windowsill overnight or put out in the noon sun for a few minutes. When shapes appeared, young girls looked for signs of what their future husbands might do for a living—a hoe, for example, might signal a farmer, or a ship might be a clue that a seaman would be her partner.

Egg yolks were also supposed to tell of future events. Many Europeans believed that a double yolk was a sign of an impending marriage. A dark spot in the yolk was a bad omen—a sign of some disaster to come. An egg without a yolk, a soft-shelled egg, and a deformed egg were all unlucky to have or behold. But it was thought one could ward off misfortune by throwing an unlucky egg over the roof of a house. Apparently there was no consideration for anyone on the other side who might have the bad luck to be in the egg's path!

Getting splattered with egg is not

> **T I D B I T**
>
> Eggs don't grow on eggplants, but the plant, a relative of the potato family, got its name from its purple fruit, which has an egglike shape.

most people's idea of fun. But several centuries ago, it was common in Scotland and Ireland to celebrate Beltane (May Day) by pelting someone with eggshells. The unlucky victim was chosen to take the place of any witch who might be around to cast evil spells. Throwing eggshells was a way to undo any damage that witchcraft might bring about.

Today, some Europeans and Americans will tell you to carefully crush eggshells; otherwise you might be subjected to some bad luck. Apparently this practice comes from the days when people believed that witches used eggshells as boats, sailing from place to place to do their mischief. But if the shells were punctured or crushed, witches had no means of transporting themselves —at least not on the sea!

Decorated Eggs

The custom of coloring or decorating eggs is ancient. For centuries, eggs were dyed with natural colorings from plants: onion skins, grass, and beets, to name a few. Roasting eggs in charcoal created black eggs, which were part of mourning ceremonies.

Red has been the most popular color for eggs because of its link with good luck and magic. In fact, since the Stone Age, people have believed that red coloring, no matter where it appeared, would help protect them from evil powers. Ancient Romans, for example, gave children red coral to guard against the evil eye, and a Roman legend says that on the day Alexander Severus was born, a hen laid a red egg, a sign foretelling his future: He would become an emperor.

Red eggs have long been an integral part of celebrations for newborn sons in China, and ancient Persians (Iranians) stained eggs red for religious celebrations. During a spring festival in eastern Europe, red-dyed eggs and herbs were placed in water, creating a good luck potion for washing. In many cultures, red eggs have signified a life-giving force, good health, and even eternal life, and wherever Easter has been celebrated throughout the world, red eggs have represented the blood of Christ.

The practice of coloring eggs at Easter may stem from the Jewish Passover observance, which commemorates the Israelites' deliverance from Egyptian bondage. Early on, a roasted egg, though not prepared during the exodus from Egypt, became an important part of the seder, or feast, at Passover. Today, as in the past, it symbolizes a burned offering—a sacrificial symbol of thanks-giving—for a new life after persecution. And in some parts of eastern Europe, Passover celebrations a century or two ago included eggs dyed with onion peels or coffee powder.

DYEING EGGS THE NATURAL WAY

IF YOU WANT TO DYE EGGS the natural way, you can use the juice of blueberries or red raspberries, dark coffee, and onion skins. For blue eggs, bring the blueberry juice to a boil in a pan. Remove from heat, then add two tablespoons of vinegar, and place four or five boiled eggs in the mixture, turning them until they are the color you want. Remove the eggs from the dye and let them dry.

Repeat the process with the raspberries for pink eggs. Coffee-colored eggs are prepared in a similar way, bringing the coffee to a boil and adding the vinegar before placing the eggs in the dye. To make yellow dye, boil onion skins in a pan of water, remove from heat, and add four to five hard-boiled eggs.

If you like green eggs, first create blue ones in the blueberry dye, then immerse the eggs in the yellow dye. Blue and yellow should produce green. But an easier way might be to boil eggs with green grass.

Since the first Christians were originally Jews and celebrated Easter on the same day as Passover, they continued their tradition of coloring eggs. Some historians theorize, however, that the custom of egg coloring has roots that extend even farther back in time, perhaps originating with a pagan spring fertility rite.

Whatever the source, egg decorating is both an art and big business. Many exquisitely decorated eggs made from wood, ivory, crystal, or other materials—including silver and gold—are now part of art collections worldwide. Some are enameled and covered with jewels and may include religious motifs, symbols of royalty, or birds, flowers, and other springlike designs. Those who practice the fine art of egg decorating may spend weeks if not months on their creations.

Ukrainian *pysanky* eggs—decorated as ornaments—are famous. These eggs are supposed to protect the world from evil, and any placed in a home could prevent disaster. If only a few eggs are decorated, evil could extend freely throughout the world, according to Ukrainian folklore. Many decorated eggs, on the other hand, are like a living chain that allows goodness and love to prevail.

The designs in Ukrainian decorated eggs are symbolic. Green, for example, symbolizes rebirth, and orange represents power and ambition. Flowers on *pysanky* eggs are signs of goodwill and charity. Wheat stalks represent wishes for a bountiful harvest, and evergreen trees symbolize long life. Storks and chickens signify fertility, and eggs with these designs are supposed to help a young couple bear children.

The commercial aspects of Easter celebrations in the United States depend a great deal on colorful Easter eggs and Easter baskets filled with hard-boiled eggs, candy eggs, and usually candy Easter bunnies or chicks. Across

the nation on Easter, thousands of kids take part in Easter Egg Hunts, trying to gather as many eggs—artificial or real—as possible. Some participate

TIDBIT

The Frankford Candy & Chocolate Company in Philadelphia is just one candy company in the United States that produces chocolate candies for Easter. Among the three hundred different kinds of Frankford chocolates produced are seventy-five million hollow milk-chocolate bunnies that hop off the assembly line each year for the Easter celebration.

in egg-rolling contests, races to see who can be the first to roll an egg along a grassy lane to a finish line. The most widely publicized egg rolling is held annually in Washington, D.C., on the South Lawn outside the White House. The children are supposed to roll eggs with a spoon but often flip them instead, launching them in the air like miniature footballs and hoping they'll land at the "goal line," where each contestant receives a wooden egg signed by the president.

DID YOU KNOW . . .

• Some of the most expensive eggs in the world are ostrich eggs, but the eggs aren't eaten. Most are hatched at ostrich farms, where

TAP 'N' CRACK

EGG TAPPING IS A CLASSIC Easter event, and in one area of Tennessee the contest has been held annually for more than 170 years. It's really a type of egg fight in which contestants challenge one another to determine who has the hardest eggs. The game of egg tapping (or egg picking as it's sometimes called) stems from an old European custom that has many variations, including contests in which kids try to break eggs on each other's foreheads.

How do you play the game today? Sit in a circle with other contestants, each with a supply of hard-boiled eggs. With one of your eggs, tap the egg of the person next to you, first at the pointed or small end, then at the rounded end, trying to crack your opponent's egg while salvaging the shell of your own. The ritual is repeated around the circle. If you are the last person with an uncracked egg, you will be declared the winner.

the big birds are raised for their meat, feathers, beaks, and other parts that have commercial value.

• It probably takes a couple of minutes for the average person to peel a hard-boiled egg. But professionals—those who work for food processors that prepare hardboiled eggs for restaurants—can handle the task in a matter of two or three seconds without leaving a scrap of the shell.

• Although some people believe brown eggs are more nutritious than white eggs and others believe that white eggs are fresher than brown eggs, both ideas are myths. Nutritionists tell us both brown and white eggs are equal in food value.

Professional Egg Peeler

CHAPTER 8

FISH BONES, WISHBONES, AND OTHER FISH AND POULTRY "MAGIC"

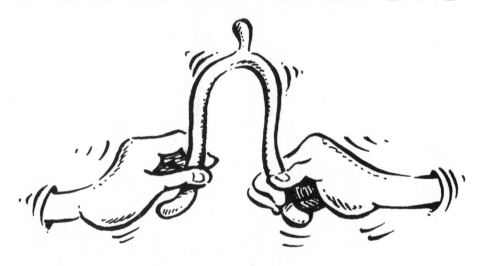

*C*HARGOGGAGOGGMANCHAUGGA-GOGGCHAUBUNAGUNGAMAUGG. It's supposed to be the longest name for any lake in the United States. But the name has been

shortened to Chaubunagungamaug on the map, and you'll find it near the southeast border of Massachusetts. Whatever people call it today, the name of the lake states the fishing rules that Native Americans lived by: "You fish your side; I fish my side; nobody fish in the middle."

Every society that has depended on lakes, inland streams, or oceans for part of its food supply developed not only rules for how and when to fish but also superstitious beliefs, and sometimes magical practices, associated with the fish and seafood caught. In some societies, fish were considered sacred and were worshiped or offered as special gifts to various gods and goddesses. Fishermen, for example, often threw the first catch back into the sea as a token to the sea god Neptune. Even today, fishermen in many parts of the world follow a similar practice in order to bring a bountiful supply of fish.

Fish are symbols of life and good luck. A great variety of fish and seafoods—from caviar (fish eggs) to pickled herring to salmon—are eaten at the beginning of a new year to ensure prosperity and to ward off misfortune during the year. In many parts of China and among U.S. citizens of Chinese ancestry, a whole fish is served for the Chinese New Year dinner, since the fish is a symbol of bounty. Where seafood is scarce, a whole fish is carved from wood and used as a table centerpiece, imparting a wish for prosperity. Shark fin soup may be served along with the fish to bring good luck for the year.

One of the most common beliefs is that fish is brain food and that children will grow in wisdom and strength if they eat fish. Some people insist that eating fish eyeballs and fish heads will increase brainpower tremendously.

While eating fish, have you ever gotten a bone caught in your throat? To remedy the problem, Hawaiians say you should put a fish bone on top of your head, then eat a lump of rice to dissolve the bone. In other parts of the United States, particularly in the South, people insist that white bread must be eaten with fish in order to prevent choking on fish bones. Both the rice and bread probably help carry a fishbone down the gullet, but there appears to be no explanation for this New England superstition: To dislodge a fishbone in your throat, yank on your big toe!

The eel, a snakelike fish, is thought to have diverse magical powers. It was an old British custom to wrap an eel skin around an arm or leg to cure a cramp or pain in a limb. A remedy for drunkenness was to put an eel in white wine before drinking it. If you eat an eel's heart, according to one superstitious belief, you may gain the power to foretell the future.

Herring is another fish with special attributes. In England it was once believed that a young girl would dream of her future husband if she ate salted herring but didn't eat or drink anything else before going to bed. Herring also was supposed to keep flies out of a building for the summer season. All you had to do was hang a herring from the ceiling on Good Friday. That trick, however, could attract a variety of other pesty creatures!

Salmon is considered lucky by some folks. In fact, Native Americans along the Pacific Northwest coast have long celebrated this fish at annual salmon bake festivals. Salmon symbolizes a bountiful food supply. But many fishermen in Scotland believe it is unlucky to mention the fish by name, so it's called "the red fish" instead. And any fisherman who brings up a salmon on his first catch, throws it back quickly because it is a sign of bad luck.

"Magic" in Shells

Shellfish, too, are surrounded by superstitious beliefs. Some people believe that crabs bring bad luck, but the Japanese consider crabs magical sea creatures. In fact, crab shells over a doorway can drive away evil spirits and keep people healthy. Clams, shrimp, lobster, and other creatures from the sea have good

HOW TO PREPARE AND EAT A LOBSTER

1. Select a lobster and drop it into a pot of boiling water.

2. After about ten minutes remove the lobster from the pot and serve.

3. Tie a large bib around your neck.

4. Twist off the claws, then use a nutcracker to crack each claw.

5. Separate the tailpiece by arching the back until it cracks.

6. Break the flippers off the tailpiece.

7. Insert a fork inside the body where the flippers broke off.

8. Pull the back from the body.

9. Open the remaining part of the body by cracking sideways and eat the meat inside.

10. Suck the meat from the small claws.

THE KILLER CONE & CRAB COMBO
(Proof that Crustaceans & Creme do _Not_ mix)

ly combination, they say, although that's been proven a myth.

Oysters, often called "manna from the sea," have been associated with a long-held superstition that it's unsafe to eat them in the months with no R—that is, from May to August. But the fact is oysters can be eaten all year long. The superstition probably came about because oysters would spoil in days past when there was no refrigeration. The summer months are also the time when female oysters spawn, producing millions of eggs during the season. So not eating oysters during those months helped keep the species alive.

OF BONES AND BIRDS

The bone next to the breast of a

and bad luck attributes. Many people believe you should never eat these foods with ice cream—a dead-

TALKING TURKEY

HAVE YOU EVER HEARD of turkeys falling over dead drunk? A folktale from Tennessee tells about such turkeys and their magical resurrection. It seems an elderly woman of the Civil War period raised turkeys for part of her food supply. Once when guests came, the old woman served a meal, then brought out a jar of cherries that she had preserved in brandy. After her guests ate the brandied cherries, the woman threw the cherry pits outdoors.

Not long afterward, she found her turkeys keeled over; they appeared to be dead. Determined not to have a total loss, the old woman plucked all of the turkeys' feathers to use as stuffing for pillows and bedding. But a few hours later, she saw the turkeys up and about, prancing around in their bare skin. She soon realized the turkeys had gotten drunk from eating the brandied cherry pits and had just passed out!

Since cold weather was coming, she had to figure out a way to keep her turkeys from freezing to death. So she made woolen jackets for all of her turkeys, which helped the entire flock survive—and saved the food supply.[10]

Garments for Gobblers

chicken, turkey, goose, or other fowl has been called the "merry thought" and the "marriage bone," but most people today think of it as the "wishbone." After carving and eating portions of a cooked bird, people often save the wishbone, allowing it to dry thoroughly before using it for a centuries-old practice: breaking the wishbone with a friend or relative, hoping that one's wish will come true.

When two people take part in this ritual, each holds an end of the wishbone between the thumb and forefinger and brings to mind a "merry thought" or makes a wish. Each person pulls on the wishbone to break it, and the one with the longest part is supposed to have her or his wish come true.

Chicken bones of all kinds have been used to predict the future. Bone divination has a long history in Asia and the Pacific Islands, as well

TIDBIT

A familiar nursery rhyme tells about "four and twenty blackbirds baked in a pie," which may seem a bit odd today. Seldom do people describe cooking or eating blackbird. But it certainly was a common practice during the 1800s in the United States. Thousands of blackbirds were captured from along the Delaware River in Pennsylvania, and the birds were fried, broiled, roasted, and served in a variety of ways at nearly every good hotel in Philadelphia.

as in some parts of Africa. To divine future events, people insert splinters of bamboo into the tiny holes that are in the bones of chickens and other fowl. The splinters extend at varied angles and distances apart, which are measured to determine what the chicken bones predict for the days, months, or years ahead.

Live chickens were also considered prophetic birds. Ancient Romans raised large flocks of chickens not only for the meat and eggs they produced but also to foretell the outcome of a battle. How? The Romans threw feed to those set aside as "holy" birds and watched to see whether some of the feed would drop from the chickens' beaks and "dance" (bounce rhythmically) on the ground. If the seed "danced," Roman soldiers could expect to win the next battle; if not, they saw it as an omen to forgo the fight.

DID YOU KNOW . . .

- It is an old British belief that a person should eat goose on Michaelmas Day, or the Festival of St. Michael, a Christian celebration held on September 29, to ensure that there will be enough money to pay debts.

- Goose Tongue has nothing to do with the bird. Instead, it's the nickname for a wild plant found in southeast Alaska along the Gulf of Alaska coast. Native Alaskans eat the green leaves of Goose Tongue either fresh or cooked.

- Chicken soup was once said to be a "magical" cure for various ailments, particularly the common cold. But the claim has little to do with magic. Scientific studies have shown that chicken soup can help clear mucus from the respiratory tract and help the body rid itself of the virus causing the infection.

CHAPTER 9

"WHERE'S THE BEEF?"

"**I** SAW SALTED HUMAN FLESH suspended from beams between the houses, just as with us it is the custom to hang bacon and pork." That's how Amerigo Vespucci, an Italian navigator from Florence, described the practices of the Tupinambas who lived along the coast of what is now Brazil. In letters written in 1505, Vespucci noted that the cannibals thought it strange that "we do not eat our enemies and do not use as food their flesh, which they say is most savory."[11]

Most of us today are repulsed by the idea of eating human flesh, but people of ancient civilizations in both South and North America viewed this practice as almost sacred, offering the best parts of a captive's flesh—often the dark thigh meat— as gifts to their rulers. Among some ancient peoples, it was a common practice to offer sacrifices of human flesh to their gods as well.

During religious rituals, people also ate a sacred animal—perhaps a bear, lion, or wolf—that represented a god. People believed that eating the flesh and drinking the blood of the animal would make them god-like. In a drastically changed form, that ritual carried over to the Christian communion that has been practiced for centuries: Bread and wine in the ceremony symbolize sacred flesh and blood.

ARE WE THE MEAT WE EAT?

One of the most widespread meat-eating superstitions in ancient times was the belief that humans took on the characteristics of animals they consumed. Native Americans, for example, believed that anyone who ate the flesh of a coyote would become a coward, and even starving people were warned to forgo coyote for dinner.

In some African tribes, it was common to eat the liver of a heroic person in order to assume that characteristic. Eating various animal organs was another way to obtain certain traits. If you accepted such a belief, you might decide to eat the heart of a lion or a wolf to gain courage. But suppose instead you decided to eat the heart of a rabbit? You might take on that animal's characteristics, running away from adversity with great speed, which might cause others to label you "timid" or "afraid."

Today, many Americans believe that they should eat red meat for strength, because such meat comes from strong animals, especially beef cattle. In fact, some ads for beef products strongly suggest that anyone who *doesn't* eat beef is a wimp! Although there's no big promotional effort for other "hearty" meats, perhaps one could also avoid wimpiness by eating the meat of oxen, buffalo, or even horses?

ANIMAL POWER

Since prehistoric times people have believed that certain animals have supernatural control over their lives. Legends, myths, and numerous superstitious practices have focused on the supposed magical powers of animals. In addition, it has been a common practice to sacrifice animals in religious ceremonies, slaughtering an ox, ram, sheep, or lamb and then preparing the meat for a community feast. But meat

T I D B I T

About 80 percent of the world's population eats insects for protein, often as a substitute for meat. While most Americans turn up their noses at the very thought of insect eating, some unbiased individuals say that such culinary treats as highly spiced pan-fried mealworms, chocolate-covered crickets and ants, and waxworm corn fritters are tasty—even delicious.

was not usually included in the everyday meals of ordinary working people or the poor; they could not afford to raise animals for meat. Some, however, could keep a pig and fatten it for butchering. A pig often foraged for its own food in the woods or roamed the village or city streets in search of garbage.

Pigs have been domesticated for thousands of years, and historians say there is evidence that the animals were raised for food in Egypt and China as long ago as 5000 b.c. Pigs were (and still are) so common that people worldwide, except for religious groups such as Jews and Muslims who forbid pork eating, have considered pork a meat with special attributes.

Ancient Greeks, Romans, Gauls, and Germans ate pork on numerous festive occasions. Not only did they enjoy it, but the pig was thought to have magical qualities. In China, people have long eaten pork on New Year's Day to ensure good luck for the year. During the Middle Ages, Viking warriors thought that if they were killed in battle they would go to a heaven where they could feast forever on the flesh of a magical boar—a wild pig that reappeared the day after it was eaten!

Pork eating has also been associated with lucky events throughout the history of the United States. Remember Hoppin' John, the good luck dish made with pork or ham described in chapter 5? But parts of pork meat may have been even more important for healing purposes. Pork and other meats were used in numerous folk remedies for ailments ranging from minor injuries like a cut to life-threatening pneumonia.

SMELLY REMEDIES

In rural America, an old method for healing a sore throat was to place bacon fat or salt pork on the throat and tie it in place with a piece of flannel or a dirty sock—the dirtier and smellier the better, according to some folks. Using another version of the remedy, some people sprinkled the pork with pepper or added onions to this "sandwich" cure.

A poultice of bacon fat was sup-

posed to heal boils, folk medicine declared. And salt pork was a common application to draw poison and infection from open wounds.

Cuts of raw beef could also be used as compresses. Putting a raw beefsteak on bruises and various skin injuries was supposed to aid in healing. Boxers often used beefsteak to diminish the swelling caused by a blow to the eye, although most professional boxers today say that the practice was based on pure superstition. Besides, they'd rather *eat* the steak!

Raw beef was also a remedy for warts. Given all the vegetable remedies available as well, it seems that lots of people were afflicted with warts. If that was the case, perhaps

they needed a variety of methods to try.

How was raw beef supposed to remove warts? One method advised burying a piece of steak where three roads meet. Another instructed: Rub the beef on the wart, wrap the meat in paper, then bury the package. A more practical idea was to throw the meat to the dog! But would that give the dog warts?

Other animal products such as bear grease, skunk oil, and snake oil were used as remedies for a variety of ailments just a few generations ago. Some of the curatives stemmed from Native American practices, which farmers, trappers, and others adapted. Today, there are questions about which old-time "cures" were

superstitious practices and which were truly effective remedies. But folks who used them in the past swore that *all* of the treatments worked.

Skunk oil (or skunk spray) was a popular curative for a number of ailments, from colds to rheumatism. But before the oil could be used, someone had to trap a skunk, kill it, then immediately "grab the skunk by the tail with one hand and the scruff of the neck with the other . . . set the skunk's bottom firmly in the torn-up dirt where the trap had been, and he would spray into it," as one trapper reported.[12]

Skunk oil and bear grease, or bear oil rendered from the fat of the animal, were often used as liniments for aching joints or just to rub into the body to improve muscle tone. Bear oil, lard, goose grease, and chicken fat—sometimes mixed with turpen-tine—were also common rubbing compounds and poultices used for chest colds.

STONE SOUP

SUPPOSE YOU WANT TO make soup or stew. You'd need vegetables and probably meat. But what happens if you don't have any of the ingredients? Should you do without? Perhaps you can try a magic trick described in a story that has been told over and over again through the centuries:

A vagrant is wandering through the countryside one day and becomes very hungry, but he has no money to buy food. So he goes to a miserly woman's house, knocks on the door, and asks to borrow a pot to make soup from a pebble he is carrying in his pocket. The woman is amazed and curious, wondering how soup can be created from just a pebble. So she fills a pot full of water and watches the water heat over an outdoor fire.

The vagrant suggests that a little meat would be good to add flavor, and the woman finds some leftovers, chops them up, and throws them in the pot. Next there's a need for potatoes, then onions, then tomatoes, and any other vegetables that might be handy, plus some salt and pepper. Each item is added to the simmering pot. When the woman finally tastes the soup, she calls it the best she's ever eaten and asks to keep the stone. Of course the vagrant obliges, telling the woman she now has the magic formula for stone soup.

(By the way, if you heard this story in Sweden, the soup would be made with a nail, a little flour, some salt-ed beef, potatoes, barley, and milk.)

Stone Soup

Rattlesnake oil was another popular liniment as well as an antidote for earache and toothache. Where did people get snake oil? Sometimes they bought it at medicine shows and fairs, but that type of snake oil was often a fake product. Folks who made the real thing had to catch a rattlesnake, then kill it, drop it in a pot of water, boil it until the fat came to the top, skim off the oil, and bottle it for future use.

DID YOU KNOW . . .

- Goats have long been considered lucky in many societies and were often kept as protective mascots for food animals, such as cattle and sheep.

- Although the hamburger tops the list of meat sandwiches sold in the United States, the frankfurter—or hot dog—is among the top ten and is one of America's favorite foods. Back in the early 1900s vendors at ballparks called the frankfurter a dachshund sausage because it looked like the long, skinny dog. While going through the stands, they cried: "Red hot dachshund

sausage! Get your red hot dachshund!" One day, a New York newspaper published a cartoon by Tad Dorgan, who created a vendor selling a barking sausage sandwich to baseball fans. Because Dorgan couldn't spell *dachshund,* he used the term *hot dog.* The name has been with us ever since.

• Horsemeat has not been an acceptable food in the United States, except when the price of beef was very high or beef was in short supply, as it was during World War I and World War II. The taboo against horsemeat may stem from the notion that it's revolting to eat an animal that is like a "friend" or family pet. But other animals, including pigs, cows, sheep, and lambs, have become pets and still end up on the dinner table!

CHAPTER 10

A DRINK TO YOUR GOOD FORTUNE!

WHEN "BUBBLE WATER," OR SELTZER, was invented in the early 1800s, it was called a "democratic drink" because it was enjoyed by both the rich and the poor. Ads for soda water claimed that just a sip of seltzer would provide a wonderful experience, "which, like the sensations of love, cannot be forgotten."[13]

WATER OF LIFE

Folklore from around the world tells of magic that comes from water—natural water, not the carbonated kind. Many ancient legends focus on a quest for the "water of life," which was thought to cure a great many illnesses, ensure eternal life, or even restore life to the dead. Remember Ponce de León, the Spanish explorer who sailed to the "new world" in search of the Fountain of Youth? Although he found plenty of water

in what is now the state of Florida, the explorer never located a source that would guarantee youth forever. Still, certain springs, fountains, wells, streams, lakes, and ponds the world over have been considered "magical" or "holy," and water from these sources has been thought to be a cure-all for numerous disorders.

Since the dawn of civilization, people have believed that water could purify as well as cure. Newborns were usually immersed in a nearby stream, lake, or pond so that they would would have a long and healthy life. This practice has carried over to baptismal rites of today. In some cultures, bathing in purifying waters is a part of other life ceremonies, such as a ritual bath for brides to wash away evil influences. People also washed dead bodies to keep away evil spirits.

To Dowse or Divine

Water is essential for life, so it is no wonder that people have always been eager to find sources of pure water. A stream or a spring that bubbles naturally from the ground can provide a ready water supply. And digging a well to tap an underground spring or aquifer is an ancient practice. But what if that underground source is difficult to find? You might need the services of a dowser—a person who locates water using a divining rod (a forked, or

V-shaped, twig usually from a witch hazel bush or a peach tree).

How does the rod work? The dowser holds on to the tips of the twig, rather like grasping a wishbone, and carries it in that manner while walking over ground where there is—the diviner hopes!—an underground water source. If the divining rod bends downward, you'd better mark the spot and start digging. Some people swear by this method. Others say it's pure superstition.

If you want to ensure that a well won't dry up, you can act on another superstitious belief. On the first day of the year, "feed" the well a bread crust.

WISHING WELLS AND FUTURES TOLD IN WATER

Have you ever thrown a penny or other coin in a fountain or pool of water while making a wish? If so, you're following an ancient superstitious practice. Because of water's "magical" powers, wishing wells, fountains, and ponds have appeared since the beginning of recorded history. And gold pieces, pebbles, and crooked pins were some common objects dropped into water for luck or to make a wish.

Today, people are encouraged to throw coins into public fountains or ornamental pools as a way to make charitable contributions. The coins are collected periodically and distributed to groups working for social and health-care causes. Sometimes homeowners create their own personal "wishing wells," constructing backyard ponds or fountains "just for luck."

Water wells can also predict the future. One common practice long ago was to drop a shirt or other piece of clothing from a sick person into a well to predict whether that person would recover or die. If the clothing floated on the water, it was a signal of healthier days ahead. You can imagine the sick person's feelings if the clothing sank to the bottom!

Dreaming about water is also supposed to portend future events, most of them unpleasant. Don't dream about drowning. Some believe that's a death omen. A waterfall in your dream is a sign that you'll run into some problems trying to accomplish a project you've undertaken. And you might as well forget starting any new project if you dream about a pool of water, which signals stagnation.

But there is an antidote for dreams of water: After such a dream, take a cold or lukewarm bath, adding some salt to the water. Perhaps a swim or dunk in salty seawater would do just as well. But you'd have to bathe again to get rid of the sticky residue on your body!

LUCKY AND PROPHETIC BREWS

Water takes on special properties when it's used to make tea or coffee. If you stir a cup of tea, coffee, or hot chocolate and see bubbles on top of the brew, you're in luck. The bubbles forming in the center indicate you'll receive money in the future, or they may be a sign of good weather

TIDBIT

A "tempest in a teapot" is an old saying that suggests a person is making a big fuss about a trivial matter.

A Tempest in a Teapot

for the day. But don't stir another person's coffee—you'll create disharmony.

Cocoa or chocolate drinks have been associated with magic and superstition for more than four thousand years. The ancient Aztecs are credited with creating a drink called *cacahuatl*, mixing ground cocoa beans with water, which they believed was the "drink of the gods." The chocolate drink was said to prolong life and to be an aphrodisiac. According to legend, one Aztec ruler consumed fifty cups of chocolate daily!

Tea is probably one of the most prophetic drinks. Making tea and reading the tea leaves at the bottom of a cup or pot are (excuse the expression) *steeped* in superstition. If you put boiling water in a teapot before putting in the tea, you're asking for misfortune. And don't drain all the water from a teakettle, because that, too, could be unlucky. When brewing tea, don't for fortune's sake forget to pour the brew—you guessed it, that could court bad luck, too.

If you accidentally make weak

tea, you could be losing a friendship; a strong brew, on the other hand, is a sign of a new friendship on the horizon. Don't stir the tea in the pot, or you'll have an argument with someone. Putting milk into tea before sugar is also a bad omen.

If you leave the top off a pot of tea, you're likely to have a visit from a stranger. Another sign that a stranger will arrive is to see a stalk (a piece of woody fiber) or a tea leaf floating on top of a cup of tea. British tea drinkers say that you can tell the day of the week the stranger will appear by placing the stalk or leaf on the back of your hand. Then you hit it with your other hand, counting each swat or saying each day of the week until the stalk or leaf sticks to your palm. When that happens, you know the day to expect the stranger.

It's a definite possibilitea.

For centuries people have claimed to read the future in tea leaves, and hundreds of books and articles have been written on the subject. People who read tea leaves begin with loose tea (not the bagged kind), placing half a teaspoon or so in a clean cup, then pouring hot water over the leaves. A rather tricky swirling and sloshing process follows, with a reader slowly rotating the cup and draining the tea into a saucer, bowl, or other container until the tea leaves stick to the cup's sides. Every tea reader has her or his own technique for this process. But the leaves that remain in the cup supposedly form in shapes that symbolize a future event.

Leaves shaped like an ax, for example, could signal danger. A car (not too surprisingly) symbolizes a trip. Gallows, as you might expect, could be a sign of serious trouble. A harp symbolizes joy, a heart supposedly means future happiness, and a wishbone indicates—what else?— that a wish will come true!

A Drink to Luck!

Numerous superstitions are associated with alcoholic beverages. Beer is one of the oldest fermented drinks and has

> **TIDBIT**
>
> At the end of the 1800s, New York City boasted more soda fountains than bars.

been considered magical for eons. Ancient Egyptians, for example, believed that a dream about drinking beer foretold joy and long life. Beer has long been part of potions designed to "cure" ailments and purify the mind of evil thoughts.

Drinking beer—and wine—has been an integral part of many harvest and religious festivals since ancient times, and over the ages people have shared drinks of beer and wine as well as other alcoholic beverages at countless social events.

On special occasions, people may toast one another with their drinks. In a toast, people raise their glasses, clink them together, and wish one another good health, good cheer, or just good luck.

There are many theories on how this ritual began. Some say it stemmed from a time when people used to poison their enemies or those they just wanted out of their way. To accomplish this, a poisonous substance was put into the potential victim's wine. So in order to avoid being poisoned, people would switch glasses of wine with each other. Then, later, they began to just clink their glasses together to drive out any evil spirits or to show that they meant no

CLINK!

HOT AND COLD—
WATER, THAT IS

HAVE YOU EVER GOTTEN into hot water—other than when you take a bath or shower? Getting into "hot water" often means you're in trouble—perhaps BIG trouble. That old saying probably came about because of an ancient safety measure. To discourage a break-in, a homeowner or store-keeper kept a pot of boiling water ready to toss at an intruder!

Throwing cold water on something or someone on a hot day may seem like fun and even a welcome act, but if you throw cold water on an idea, that's a different matter. Usually that means you're trying to discourage some project or event that's in the planning stages. It's similar to "raining on someone's parade."

IN HOT WATER   OUT IN THE COLD

harm to one another.

Another theory suggests that toasting originated with the ancient practice of making offerings to deities to

prevent misfortune. People offered drinks and food as they chanted special requests, asking that they or their friends and family be spared from evil or bad luck. Perhaps that's the reason an old Irish toast makes a plea for another person's welfare: "May you be in heaven a half hour before the devil knows you're dead!"

Another common drinking ritual today is blowing foam off a glass of beer just after it's poured. That's supposed to bring good luck. If a little beer is spilled, not to worry, because that's also good luck. Spilling wine, on the other hand, is a sign that misfortune lies in wait. But you can undo that bad luck by dipping a finger in the wine and rubbing it behind your ear.

DID YOU KNOW . . .

• The term *cocktail* may have originated with the British, who made a drink called "cock ale." Apparently a large rooster (cock) was cut up and boiled, then steeped in a barrel of ale, raisins, and spices for a week or so before the concoction was bottled.

• Wines have been made from a great variety of fruits and seeds, but ancient Romans made grape wine famous, selling it to people such as the British who had never before drunk wine. Roman wines were often flavored with flowers, herbs, and honey.

CHAPTER 11

COINS IN CAKES AND FORTUNES IN COOKIES

"HAPPY BIRTHDAY TO YOU, HAPPY birthday to you . . ." The song usually begins the ritual. The candles on your birthday cake burn brightly, and while making a wish, you try to blow out each and every flame in one long exhaled breath. If all the candles go out, your wish will come true.

Your cake might also have a "Happy Birthday" greeting written in the icing. If you eat part of the greeting, you help ensure a happy event. The practice comes from old rituals and beliefs of various religions that eating food with a message written on it gives a person the power of the inscribed words.

The birthday cake is just one of many ways that people use cakes, pastries, sweet breads, puddings, and other dessert foods to help celebrate special occasions and at the same time try to ensure good fortune. The wedding cake and the ceremonies associated with it, for example, have long symbolized special good luck wishes. The wedding "cake" was once made of bread, which was broken over the bride's head to guarantee fertility and wealth. The crumbs, in turn, brought good luck to the guests who gathered up their share and sprinkled themselves with bits of bread. Today, custom has the bride and groom cut the first piece of cake to ensure that their marriage will be fruitful. And guests at some weddings take home pieces of wedding cake for luck.

Since ancient times in many cultures, cakes of various kinds have been offered to spirits of the dead—so they will have good fortune and a food supply for the afterlife. Burial

cakes are still placed beside the dead in some funeral ceremonies today. They also are part of All Souls' Day, a celebration of the dead that in Mexican tradition begins on October 31 to commemorate children who have died and extends into the next day to honor older souls. Ornately decorated sweet breads are often shaped into the form of a person or baked in rounds or loaves with ceramic heads stuck into the surfaces to honor the dead.

Another age-old practice is to place a charm—a ring, coin, button, thimble, or other object—inside a dessert. If your portion contains the charm, good luck is coming your way.

Certain holidays require "charmed" foods. On Shrove Tuesday, the day

before Lent begins in the Christian calendar, many people make pancakes, dropping a coin or ring in the batter. When the pancakes come off the griddle, any single person who gets the charm will marry soon, according to superstition. Whether you get a charm or not, eating pancakes on Shrove Tuesday brings good fortune. But you have to make a pancake for yourself, flip it on the griddle, and then eat it to get the luck.

CHRISTMAS AND NEW YEAR "PLUMS"

Little Jack Horner
sat in a corner
Eating a Christmas pie.
He stuck in his thumb
and pulled out a plum
And said, "What a brave boy
am I!"

Jack Horner in the old nursery rhyme might have been considered brave (although some versions of the verse say he was "good" rather than "brave"). For children's parties in England, it was once customary to put a plum (or prize),

> **T I D B I T**
>
> Cakes have long been given as prizes for competitions, and the phrase "to take the cake" means that someone has won honors or excelled in something.

which was attached to a string, inside a pie. A child pulled on the string to retrieve the "plum." But on some occasions a prankster might have placed a small explosive cap—like a firecracker—inside the pie. So it would have been "brave" indeed to pull out the plum!

Christmas pies, cakes, and puddings also have been made with lucky charms inside, and they are a special part of Christmas celebrations, particularly for Europeans. Charms are traditionally added to Christmas pudding, for example. Usually the charms are sterilized, perhaps wrapped in paper, and then put into the pudding. A ring symbolizes a marriage soon, a plain button means that no marriage will occur in the near future, and a coin signals that the recipient will soon enjoy wealth. To prevent misfortune, everyone in the household where the pudding is prepared has to take a turn at stirring the pudding while it cooks.

Another custom during the Christmas season is to bake a cake for Christmas Eve. It's considered bad luck to cut or serve the cake before that time, and a portion of the cake has to be saved for Christmas Day to prevent misfortune for the coming year.

Mince pie may be even more important to Christmas and New Year luck. Advice that has been passed on for centuries is to taste a mince pie each of the twelve days of Christmas, from December 25 to January 6. Having a taste of the same pie doesn't count. You must have a bite of a different pie each of the twelve days; that ensures good fortune for each month of the coming year.

New Year's Eve and New Year's Day are times for lucky cakes and pastries. Many Europeans believe that giving cakes away at the start of a new year helps drive bad luck or misfortune away. Pancakes also are made and tossed to bring good luck for the year.

FORTUNES IN COOKIES

Almost everyone who eats in a Chinese restaurant in the United

States expects to receive a fortune cookie to bring the meal to a happy end. But many of today's fortune cookies no longer contain messages predicting future events. Instead, the messages may be wise sayings, bits of philosophy, or advice. The next time you open a fortune cookie, you might find a message like one of these:

- *You have a friendly heart and are much admired.*

- *Life's rewards will be yours.*

- *You will take a chance on something in the near future.*

- *The current year will bring you great happiness.*

- *Your love life will be happy and harmonious.*

- *If you don't determine your own fate, it will be determined for you.*

Where do these messages come from? Years ago, fortunes were repetitions of the wise words of Confucius, some of the wisdom of Benjamin Franklin, or maxims by Aesop. But today, most fortunes are written by employees of companies like Cosmos Enterprises of Westborough, Massachusetts, which specializes in "fortune-telling," compiling a computer database of thousands of sayings printed in English, Chinese, German, Hebrew, French, and other languages. Cookie makers buy the fortunes by the millions, and they may stuff the same message inside hundreds if not thousands of cookies.

COOKIE MAKERS

Fortune cookies are an American invention, and until just a few decades ago were made by hand, with each fortune individually placed inside a cookie. During the 1960s, Edward Louie, cofounder with his father and brother of the Lotus Fortune Cookie Company in San Francisco, wanted to find an easier way to stuff thousands of fortunes inside cookies each day. For nearly twenty years family members who worked at the company had used chopsticks to flip and fold the cookies produced at the company. Louie invented a machine in 1967 that automatically inserted the slips of paper into the cookies.

Today, at the Lotus Company and in other plants where fortune cookies are made on a large scale, nearly all operations are performed by machines. The cookie batter, which usually consists of flour, sugar, vegetable oil, vanilla, and yellow food coloring, is mixed in a large machine and then pumped onto small griddles that circulate through ovens. After the cookies are baked, they look somewhat like pancakes. While they are still hot and soft, they go through a folding machine that also

> **TIDBIT**
>
> Every day, Americans break open about two million fortune cookies.

inserts the pieces of paper with fortunes or sayings on them. The cookies cool and harden in a few minutes and are carried by conveyor belts to a sorting and packaging area and then shipped to wholesalers.

Some cookie makers produce cookies in a variety of flavors—would you believe barbecue or a cheese-and-nacho fortune cookie? Some are dipped in chocolate, and colors are added to cookies for holidays, such as red and green for Christmas. There are also fortune cookies for weddings and bar mitzvahs. A fairly recent innovation is putting "lucky" numbers inside fortune cookies, which are sold in places where lottery tickets are available.

Some companies produce special orders for those big spenders who can afford to buy (and give away) cookies stuffed with jewelry or money. And most plants create promotional messages for various companies that distribute fortune cookies to prospective clients or customers.

One of the largest makers of fortune cookies today is Won Ton of Brooklyn, New York, which produces about one million cookies every day.

Fortune Cookie:

You have a friendly heart and are much admired.

Unfortunate Cookie:

You are well liked despite your table manners.

In late 1992, the company made arrangements to build and operate fortune cookie plants in China, for the first time providing these cookies on a large scale to the Chinese people.

DID YOU KNOW . . .

• A take-out restaurant in Portland, Oregon, serves "unfortunate" cookies that contain such messages as "You are well liked despite your table manners," "Your charms will persuade others to screen their calls," and "You are in your own way; please stand aside." Although most customers reportedly like the jibes, a few have been so insulted they have refused to return to the restaurant.

• In the familiar nursery rhyme about Tom, the piper's son who "stole a pig," the "pig" was actually a nickname for a fruit-filled pastry shaped like the animal. The verse says "the pig was eat/And Tom was beat/And Tom went howling down the street." At least he got his "just desert"— he was punished for his crime! Tom's punishment, though, has not been as well remembered as the pastry he stole and ate.

• More than a century ago in the southern United States, African-Americans often held a contest called a cakewalk. The winning contestant received a cake for carrying a bucket of water atop the head without spilling a drop. Many who did the cakewalk used fancy, strutting steps that eventually were incorporated into a dance called the cakewalk.

CHAPTER 12

TABLE TALK

Don't bite off more than you can chew.
Don't spill the beans.
Don't cook your own goose.

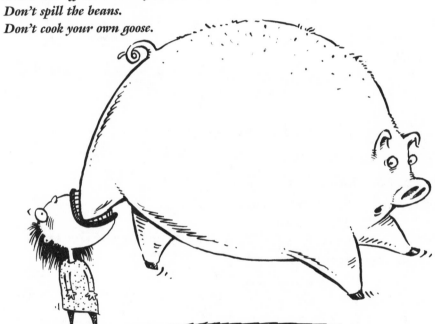

BETTY BIT OFF MORE THAN SHE COULD CHEW.

PERHAPS YOU HAVE HEARD STATEMENTS like these during "table talk" at mealtime or other occasions. If the advice is directed your way, you probably know that you're being told not

to take on more work or duties than you can handle, to keep a secret,

and, finally, not to act against your own best interests.

Humble Pie

Many bits of advice and wise sayings are connected with eating and drinking. But the words usually are not meant to be taken literally. Rather, like the "fruitful phrases" (see chapter 4), the expressions are metaphors or indirect references to eating and drinking. Can you figure out the meaning of the following sayings?

1. She'll have to eat humble pie.

2. He can't cut the mustard.

3. We're in a fine kettle of fish.

4. I'm in a pickle.

5. We have a bone to pick with you.

6. They're riding the gravy train.

7. I have egg on my face.

8. That's small potatoes.

9. Don't argue with your bread and butter.

TRANSLATIONS: (1) She'll have to apologize profusely; (2) He isn't able to accomplish a specific task; (3) We're in a terrible mess—deep trouble; (4) I'm in a dilemma; (5) They have to settle a difference of opinion with you; (6) They're living in wealth and luxury; (7) I'm embarrassed; (8) That's of little value or significance; (9) Don't do something foolish that will destroy or ruin your prospects for good fortune.[14]

"WE HAVE A BONE TO PICK WITH YOU."

BEWARE SOME TABLEWARE

Along with eating and drinking metaphors, there are numerous chants, verses, and sayings about superstitious practices connected with tableware:

> *Knife falls,*
> *gentleman calls;*
> *Fork falls,*
> *lady calls;*
> *Spoon falls,*
> *baby calls.*
> *Stir with a knife,*
> *Stir up strife.*

> *Stir with a fork,*
> *Stir up talk.*

The spoon is said to be a dangerous implement. Some people insist that you should never use your left hand to stir a spoon in a cup—unless you want to lose seven years of your life! And if a spoon should fall from your cup? Right-side-up it portends misfortune. But if the spoon lands upside down, you have a surprise in store.

Some people believe that when a baby takes a spoon for the first time, the child signals whether she or he will be left-handed or right-handed. Grabbing a spoon with the right hand is supposed to be a sign of good fortune, but grabbing with the left hand could mean trouble ahead. A lot of left-handers would strongly disagree with such a prediction and perhaps quote a popular saying: "Lefties know how to do it right!"

If you should happen to see a spoon while out for a walk or bicycle ride, leave the spoon on the ground. It may be an unfavorable omen: Some people throw a spoon away when they're having bad luck, hoping that anyone who finds the spoon will pick it up and carry off misfortune.

Of all utensils connected with food, knives probably have generated the most folk sayings and superstitions. According to one old

belief, it's unlucky to slice a loaf of bread or stick it with a knife. Apparently, that myth has been punctured: It's now common practice to slice bread at mealtime.

> **TIDBIT**
>
> A Turkish proverb reminds us that "A wound from a knife heals; that from a tongue never."

(like a paring knife or a carving knife) on the road or in a field—to find one is a portent of misfortune.

If a knife falls on the ground, it signifies bad luck to the person who dropped it. But unlike a spoon, a knife will bring good luck to anyone who finds it, some people say. Others disagree and believe that finding a knife is bad luck.

Even though there are arguments over how knives bring good or bad luck, you might be able to avoid bad luck associated with knives by following these rules:

Don't go looking for a sharp knife

Don't use a knife to spear a piece of bread and pass it to someone else. If you do, you're destined to suffer some adversity, the superstitious say.

Don't give a knife of any kind as a present, because it severs friendship or love. But if you insist on such a gift, also give a small coin, since that breaks the bad luck spell. Another version of this remedy is to ask the recipient to give you a coin—simply a token in exchange for the knife.

Don't play "spin-the-knife" or

unthinkingly spin a knife around on the table, because when the knife stops, the blade could point at someone, signaling that person's death.

Don't cross a knife and fork on your plate. Crossed utensils supposedly will bring sorrow or misfortune or spark an argument. But you can prevent any ill effects if you pick up the knife and, while holding it vertically, tap the handle end on the table three times. Or, as some superstitious folks have done, you could throw the offending knife on the floor. You'd be wise, however, to explain your actions to those unfamiliar with such practices. Otherwise you might be considered a bit peculiar!

To simplify matters, lay your knife and fork side by side on your plate. Then you won't have to worry about warding off ill effects.

SING BEFORE BREAKFAST . . .

And you'll cry before you sleep. At least that's what one superstition associated with a mealtime tells us. Another old saying advises: "Don't shake hands over the breakfast table." It's an unlucky greeting.

Take precautions, too, that you don't accidentally knock over a chair when you leave the table. That's an unlucky sign. Another bad omen is to sit next to an empty chair.

It's common knowledge that the number thirteen symbolizes bad luck. So it's probably no surprise that many people object to thirteen individuals eating at the same table. Not only is the number unlucky, it also means, in superstitious lore, that one of the thirteen will die within the year.

If you want to eat with a group, try joining a party of six. A total of seven people is considered, by some, to be the luckiest number to eat together. But watch out! There might be someone at the table who believes that *any* uneven number of people at a table is unlucky. Maybe it would help to place an extra chair at the table. But then, who's going to sit next to the "bad omen"? Anyone for musical chairs?

While eating, be careful that you don't drop anything. Remember that bread dropped with the buttered side down is a bad omen. If you drop any food from your fork, that's unlucky, too.

Bad luck also comes to anyone who takes the last slice of bread or cake, or the last cookie from a plate. But there's a way to prevent misfortune. You can toss a bread slice or cookie in the air before eating it. Apparently there is no antidote for the last piece of cake. You could *try*

tossing it, but chances are you'd end up with a crumbly mess on your head or in your lap!

If you have pie for dessert, the way a slice is placed foretells certain events. If the point is toward you, you'll receive a letter. A slice of pie turned sideways means you'll get a package. Nothing at all happens if the pie points away from you, except

that you'll probably enjoy the dessert when you eat it!

What if there are leftovers after a meal? Well, don't leave them on the table overnight. As you might guess, it's bad luck (and not a very healthful practice either, since some foods spoil without refrigeration). If you give any leftovers away, don't forget to tell the recipient to return your food container unwashed. Washing can destroy the luck associated with the food. It's okay, though, for the recipient to wash a container if it's then sent back to you with food inside.

If you happen to be a guest for a meal at someone's home for the first time, be careful what you do with the napkin and how you place your chair after you finish eating. Don't fold the napkin and don't push the chair in underneath the table. Both actions signal that you won't be asked to return for another meal.

You will depart on a more positive note, however, if you don't leave any food on your plate. "Waste not, want not" is an old saying, implying that anyone who wastes food is committing a grave sin. So if you want to ensure that luck and all good things come your way, eat your broccoli, brussels sprouts, rutabaga, spinach, turnips—or whatever.

DID YOU KNOW . . .

• People used spoons or similar scooped implements long before they fashioned forks for themselves. The first forks, historians say, were probably patterned after forked sticks that were used for

The Cro-Magnon Cafeteria

such purposes as spearing fish or cultivating the ground. In times past, people considered the fork a sacred implement and sometimes buried it near courtyard or city walls to keep negative or evil forces at bay.

• Until about the eleventh century in Europe, most people ate with their fingers. This is still a common practice in some parts of the world.

CHAPTER 13

ARE YOU SUPERSTITIOUS?

MOST OF US CLAIM WE AREN'T superstitious, but worldwide every group of people has followed some superstitious—or magical—practice. One of the oldest and most widespread is to avoid anything to do with the number thirteen, which is supposed to be unlucky. So if you decide to skip this short thirteenth chapter, that's okay. Or you might decide, instead, to defy this bad luck omen and look over the summary of foods below; they've been selected because they're supposed to have magical benefits. There are lucky foods for each month of the year, plus another for good measure:

January	*Black-eyed peas*
February	*Noodles (for the lunar New Year)*
March	*Seeds (like sunflower or pumpkin) or sprouts*
April	*Eggs (in any form, even raw)*
May	*Yogurt or cheese*
June	*Wedding cake*
July	*Watermelon*
August	*Corn on the cob*
September	*Oysters or fish*
October	*Pumpkin pie*
November	*Turkey*
December	*Fruit or mincemeat pie*

For an extra advantage, eat honey any time of the year—it's supposed to be one of the most "magical" foods around!

If you feel the need for more foods to boost your fortunes, try ice cream and chocolate. Both are known as "comfort foods"—they make most of us feel good. Some say ice cream is also a food that enhances love. And chocolate has long been associated with wealth. So if you top off a meal with a chocolate sundae, who can blame you? Just remember to use some restraint: Eating ice cream and chocolate every day adds heavy-duty fat and calories to your diet and perhaps pounds to your body—unless of course you believe in "magical" remedies to take off weight. But then, you aren't superstitious, are you?

SOURCE NOTES

1. Ernest Sutherland Bates, ed., *The Bible as Literature* (New York: Simon & Schuster, 1957), p. 95.

2. Martin Elkort, *The Secret Life of Food* (Los Angeles: Jeremy P. Tarcher, 1991), p. 150.

3. Dee Coutelle, *The Perfect Croissant* (Chicago: Contemporary Books, 1983), Introduction, pp. v—vi.

4. Quoted in Iona Opie and Moira Tatem, eds., *A Dictionary of Superstitions* (Oxford and New York: Oxford University Press, 1989), p. 3.

5. Adapted from William D. Westervelt, collector and translator, *Hawaiian Legends of Ghosts and Ghost-Gods* (Rutland, Vt.: Charles E. Tuttle, 1963, 1991).

6. 2 Kings 20:7.

7. Ann Kondo Corum, *Folk Wisdom From Hawaii* (Honolulu, Hawaii: Bess Press, 1985), p. 60.

8. Adapted from Charles Camp, *American Foodways* (Little Rock, Ark.: August House Publishers, 1989), pp. 31—32.

9. Sophie Hodorowicz Knab, *Polish Customs, Traditions, & Folklore* (New York: Hippocrene Books, 1993), p. 249.

10. Adapted from Kemp P. Battle, *Great American Folklore* (Garden City, NY: Doubleday & Co., 1986), pp. 560—61.

11. Quoted in Betty Fussell, *The Story of Corn* (New York, Alfred A. Knopf, 1992), p. 38.

12. Quoted in Elisabeth Janos, *Country Folk Medicine* (Chester, Conn.: The Globe Pequot Press, 1990), p. 14.

13. Quoted in Molly O'Neill, *New York Cookbook* (New York: Workman Publishing, 1992), p. 196.

14. Adapted from Charles Earle Funk, *2107 Curious Word Origins, Sayings, and Expressions* (New York: Galahad Books), 1993.

INDEX

Page numbers in italics indicate boxed text and "Tidbits."

Potatoes, 34–35, 39
Prophetic brews, 72–73
Pumpkin pie, 3
Pumpkins, *33, 34*

Rattlesnake oil, 67
Red coloring, 49
Religious rituals, 78
    animals in, 62, 63
Rituals
    bread, 9–10
    harvest, 3, 4
    religious, 62, 63, 78
    symbolic, 15–16
Romans, 3, 13, 16, 42, 49, 59, 63
    wines, 76
Rue, 16

St. Patrick's Day, 2, 31
Salmon, 56
Salt mines, *14*
Salt superstitions, 12–15, 42
Sandwiches, *7*
Sauerkraut, 29
Scotland, 7, 8–9, 14, 49, 56
Seafood, 55, 56–57
Seder, 9, 49
Seeds, magical, 19–20, 23, 26
Seltzer, 69
Shellfish superstitions, 56–57
Shortbread, 9
Shrove Tuesday, 79
Skunk oil, 65–66
Social customs
    bread in, 8, 10
    salt in/and, 14–15
Soda fountains, *74*
Spinach, 37
Spoon(s), 87–88, 92
Sri Lanka, 41
Stone Soup, *66*
Symbolism
    of bread, 10–11
    of eggs, 47, 51

of fish, 55
of fruits, 26
of herbs, 15–16

Table talk, 85–93
Tableware, 87–90, 92–93
Tangerines, 23
Tea, 72–73
Tea leaves, 72, 73
Thanksgiving, 3
Toasts, toasting, 74–76
Tomatoes, 24, 31–32
Tupinambas (people), 61–62
Turkeys, 3, *58*
Turks, 11, 16
Tussie-mussies, 17

Ukrainian *pysanky* eggs, 50–51

Valentine's Day, 2
Vegetable superstitions, 29–39
Vegetables
    as cures, 34–37
Vespucci, Amerigo, 61–62
Vienna, 11
Vikings, 64

Walnuts, 26, 27
Warts, 34, 64–65
Wassailing, 2
Water, 69–72
    hot/cold, *75*
Watermelon, 22–23
Weaning, 41
Weather, 2, 42
Wedding cake, 78
Wells, 71
Wines, 74, 76
Wishbone, 59
Wishing wells, 71
Won Ton (co.), 82–84
"Worth your salt," 14

Yeast, 10
Yogurt, 41, 43–44, *43*